COLUMBIA COLLEGE

3 2711 00015 4605

D1788981

ENTERED FEB 2 8 1994

Wounded Knee
Lest We Forget

Alvin M. Josephy, Jr.

Trudy Thomas

& Jeanne Eder

**Introductory Essay by
George P. Horse Capture**
Second Edition, Revised

International Standard Book Number: 0931618452
Library of Congress Catalog Card Number: 90-84774

© 1993 by Buffalo Bill Historical Center. All rights reserved. No part of this book may be reproduced without the written permission of the Buffalo Bill Historical Center. First edition published 1990. Second Edition 1993.

Both editions were printed by Artcraft Printers, Billings, Montana.

The first edition was published in conjunction with the exhibition WOUNDED KNEE: Lest We Forget The exhibition was on view at the Buffalo Bill Historical Center, Cody, Wyoming, from September 17, 1990 through November 30, 1990, and at the Robinson State Museum/Cultural Heritage Center, South Dakota State Historical Society, Pierre, South Dakota, from December 15, 1990 through March 15, 1991.

The exhibition was funded in part by a grant from the ARCO Foundation, the DeWitt Dominick Memorial Fund and the National Endowment for the Humanities, a federal agency.

Exhibition and Publications Designer: Robert Weiglein
Editor: Frances B. Clymer
In-house Photography: Robert Weiglein

Cover: *Big Foot Frozen in Death at Wounded Knee, January 1, 1891.*
Photographer: Clarence Grant Morledge.
Courtesy Paul and Teresa Harbaugh.

```
973.86 J83w 1993

Josephy, Alvin M., 1915-

Wounded Knee
```

BUFFALO BILL HISTORICAL CENTER

BOARD OF TRUSTEES

Mrs. Henry H.R. Coe
Chairman
Cody, Wyoming

Ernest J. Goppert, Jr.
Vice Chairman and Secretary
Cody, Wyoming

Charles G. Kepler
Vice Chairman and Treasurer
Cody, Wyoming

Jesse M. Taggart
Vice Chairman
Cody, Wyoming

Henry H.R. Coe, Jr.
Assistant Secretary
Cody, Wyoming

William C. Garlow
Assistant Secretary and Assistant Treasurer
Cody, Wyoming

Arthur D. Amiotte
Custer, South Dakota

Paul R. Brenner
New York, New York

George Brown
Cody, Wyoming

D. Harold Byrd, Jr.
Dallas, Texas

Richard J. Cashman
Minneapolis, Minnesota

Silas S. Cathcart
Chicago, Illinois

Barron G. Collier, II
Cody, Wyoming

Nancy-Carroll Draper
Cody, Wyoming

Charles W. Duncan, Jr.
Houston, Texas

William C. Foxley
La Jolla, California

Curt E. Gowdy
Boston, Massachusetts

Donald W. Griffin
Wilton, Connecticut

Hon. Clifford P. Hansen
Jackson, Wyoming

Ray L. Hunt
Dallas, Texas

Joseph W. Jones
Atlanta, Georgia

H. Peter Kriendler
New York, New York

James B. Minter
Cody, Wyoming

James E. Nielson
Cody, Wyoming

Byron L. Ramsing
Palm Beach, Florida

William B. Ruger
Newport, New Hampshire

Richard J. Schwartz
Scarborough, New York

William Self
Los Angeles, California

J. Laurence Sheerin
San Antonio, Texas

Hon. Alan K. Simpson
Cody, Wyoming

John C. Sullivan
Livingston, Montana

William E. Talley
Bermuda Dunes, California

Harold R. Tate
Salt Lake City, Utah

C.E. Webster
Cody, Wyoming

William D. Weiss
Jackson, Wyoming

Emeritus trustees

Richard I. Frost
Cody, Wyoming

William H. Hornby
Denver, Colorado

Glenn E. Nielson
Cody, Wyoming

Sam H. Rosenthal
Encino, California

Hon. Milward L. Simpson
Cody, Wyoming

H.A. True, Jr.
Casper, Wyoming

PLAINS INDIAN MUSEUM ADVISORY BOARD

Silas S. Cathcart
Chairman
Chicago, Illinois

Arthur D. Amiotte
Custer, South Dakota

Garrett E. Goggles
Fort Washakie, Wyoming

Margo Grant
New York, New York

Douglas L. Manship, Sr.
Baton Rouge, Louisiana

Joe Medicine Crow
Lodge Grass, Montana

Lloyd New
Santa Fe, New Mexico

Merlin Olsen
San Marino, California

Harold Ramser
Murrieta, California

Kenneth Ryan
Box Elder, Montana

Harriet Spencer
Long Lake, Minnesota

Darwin St. Clair
Fort Washakie, Wyoming

FOREWORD

Tragedies happen every day. Some are more momentous than others. Some even get into the history books. But most do not. They are forgotten through human indifference or lost to the numbing and healing forces of time. It is even more rare that human tragedy becomes the subject for a museum exhibition. Most museums are conditioned somehow to search for beauty rather than anguish, to reveal truth rather than deceit and to celebrate the high points of history rather than the depths of infamy.

In 1890, on a cold December day in Wounded Knee, South Dakota, a human tragedy occurred which has neither since been forgotten not lost its poignancy. It was a day for Sioux people particularly and for American Indians in general that has echoed its angst through time.

The purpose of this catalogue and its companion exhibition is to explore and expose the broadest possible historical dimensions related to the incident at Wounded Knee. The sharp paradoxes subsumed in the beauty of the Ghost Dance ceremony counterposed with the carnage of the attendant massacre provide the most startling elements of this exhibition. Yet there are also many subtle shades of irony and pathos that colored that tragedy and give shape and definition to our show. The timelessness of the event reveals itself in the end with the string of telling commentaries collected from interviews with some descendants of the survivors. In all, the effort here is to unfold the true story, separate beauty from infamy and realize that, when the smoke had cleared from the last rifle and Hotchkiss cannon, a tragedy of uncommon and unforgettable proportions had taken place . . . one that would and should never recede from our national conscience.

For helping to reveal and preserve the complexities of the event and its aftermath, we owe special thanks and recognition to George Horse Capture, former Curator of the Plains Indian Museum. His organization of this exhibition, selection of objects and insightful introduction, provide a broader understanding of those tumultuous times. We are indebted also to the many museums and private collections who helped by graciously consenting to lend objects to the exhibition. We are also indebted to many members of the Indian community for their support, including Emma Plume-Clifford for her extensive assistance in the organization and research of the exhibition and Claudia Iron Hawk Sully and Mike Her Many Horses for their many hours of help. Jeanne Eder has astutely edited the many interviews among Sioux people who are descendants of survivors of Wounded Knee. We are grateful for her assistance and equally grateful to Alvin M. Josephy, Jr. for providing the thorough and provocative historical overview and Trudy Thomas for her artistic analysis of the Ghost Dance. Others who have provided valuable assistance include Forrest Fenn, Joel and Kate Kopp, Nancy O. Lurie, Nedra Matteucci, Richard A. Pohrt, Paula Richards and Hayes Otoupalik. Photographs have been provided by Paul Harbaugh and Robert Weiglein.

The exhibition was originally hosted by the Buffalo Bill Historical Center in 1990. It was funded in part by a grant from the ARCO Foundation, the DeWitt Dominick Memorial Fund and the National Endowment for the Humanities, a federal Agency.

The original exhibition catalogue sold out in less than three years, a testament to an interest in this event which appears to be growing rather than ebbing. We are pleased to again be able to offer this book to the public, in the hope that it will reach an even greater audience as time passes.

Peter H. Hassrick
Director
Buffalo Bill Historical Center

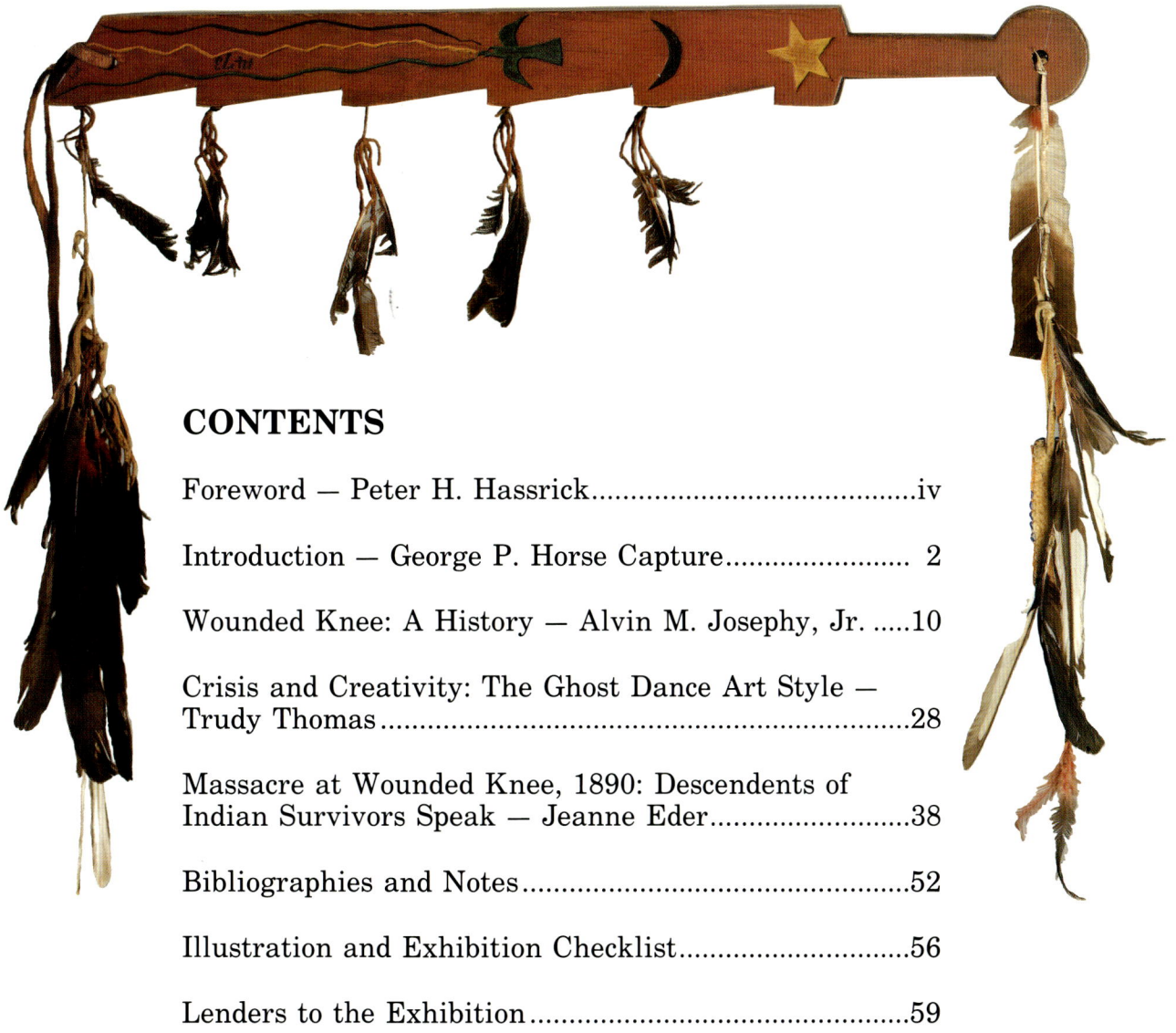

CONTENTS

Foreword — Peter H. Hassrick iv

Introduction — George P. Horse Capture 2

Wounded Knee: A History — Alvin M. Josephy, Jr. 10

Crisis and Creativity: The Ghost Dance Art Style —
Trudy Thomas 28

Massacre at Wounded Knee, 1890: Descendents of
Indian Survivors Speak — Jeanne Eder 38

Bibliographies and Notes 52

Illustration and Exhibition Checklist 56

Lenders to the Exhibition 59

1. *Quirt or Dance Wand, Cheyenne/Arapaho, c. 1891.*

2. Shirt, deerskin, Arapaho, c. 1890.

WOUNDED KNEE: THE ENDURING TRAGEDY

A Common History

Since 1492, America has been made up of groups of minority peoples, with that designation periodically shifting drastically over the years. Most of these groups melded together either genetically or, at the very least, through a common religion or a uniting philosophy of values. The majority of the unique cultural traits from these groups was sacrificed to the great American melding pot.

Many American Indians were never blended into the pot, and today they still maintain many aspects of their ancient ways. Because they are unique and separate from the mainstream, the native people are often the subject of impolite curiosity, or even suspicion by non-Indians. Their land, water, mineral and treaty rights are frequently attacked and challenged.

All and more of these forces keep the American Indian people more together than any other minority group, even though they are a minority among the minorities. As members of a close-knit group the tribes are fully aware of the common history they share; for as natives of this country they have been viewed and treated as one by the outsiders in a common "Indian-policy." In a symbolic and an actual sense, then, whatever happened to one of the tribes, happened to all of them.

Indians know of King Philip of the Wampanoags, Crazy Horse of the Sioux, Cochise of the Apache, Chief Joseph of the Nez Perce, Captain Jack of the Modocs, and all the other patriots who fought to protect their country as best they could. They share the agony of the killing fields of the Washita, Sand Creek, and Baker's massacres, as well as many others where their people died by the hundreds, women and children included. They rejoice in their victories, such as when Red Cloud closed the Bozeman Trail, when Chief Joseph and his small group fought the U.S. Army to a draw, and when Custer earned his arrow shirt. And they also know of Wounded Knee.

As an Indian person in a white world, it becomes frustrating to see non-Indians view the past and what happened to the Indian people in the abstract, or as a romantic fantasy complete with feathered warriors, galloping ponies, and bugles blowing across the plains. Many condescendingly proclaim that whatever happened was probably too bad for the Indians, but the land had to be settled and made to produce; and, anyway, that happened long ago and there is nothing that can be done about it today. Those of us who live in Indian country know this is but wishful thinking. Atrocities are still happening, the Indian people are still under siege, and the non-Indian people today could do something about these injustices. All people must know this truth.

Wounded Knee: Lest We Forget — the Project

Anyone who is in any way familiar with the Indian world is aware of the so-called Battle of Wounded Knee in 1890. In the flurry of state centennial celebrations in Indian country, the 100-year anniversary of that Indian tragedy takes on an increasing importance as a balance to the total history. As the western states of Montana, South Dakota and Wyoming mark their "winning" of the West, the commemoration of Wounded Knee is important to remind everyone that these "battles" were won at a critical cost to the Indian people who were trying to protect their country from the outside invaders.

Two years ago, our museum began to look into the possibility of presenting an exhibit featuring the Ghost Dance and Wounded Knee, to add an Indian element to the other centennials. The Plains Indian Museum is an art museum and the art of the Ghost Dance, as seen on deerskin and muslin clothing items, easily satisfies our responsibility to our artistic and Plains Indian focus.

Contact was reestablished with some Sioux friends, and we discussed the viability of such an effort. The exhibit would also tell the story of Wounded Knee, and would allow others to realize that the forces that created that horror are still with us. The concept was strengthened by their enthusiasm, but we acknowledged that we had to work with several immutable conditions: the subject and materials would be both sensitive and controversial, so we had to be perceptive and cautious; working among a tribe other than my own would present additional obstacles; the project must be endorsed, or sanctioned, by a functioning tribal entity to make it legitimate; we had to include as many other Sioux people in this project as possible, and the Sioux people must somehow directly benefit from the effort; and, finally, we had to take precautions so the project would not become a political issue among tribal factions, or the tribal governments. One thought stood above everything else—this is an important story, not only in the history of the Sioux people, but to all the Indian people, and it must be told—the truth must be known.

In 1989 we received a planning grant from the National Endowment for the Humanities, and work began in earnest. The plan was composed of a number of parts. One basic part was this publication, another, the actual exhibit. In the catalogue, the well-known and respected historian and author, Alvin M. Josephy, Jr., would provide an overview of the Wounded Knee situation as viewed by the general public. The art styles of the Ghost Dance religion would be discussed in an essay by Dr. Trudy Thomas, Curator of Fine Arts at the Museum of Northern Arizona, who chose that very topic for her successful Ph.D. dissertation. The third element of the catalogue would be most special and would tell the contemporary Sioux peoples' own story of the Wounded Knee Massacre as recollected through oral tradition. Toward this end, Mike Her Many Horses, from Wounded Knee, and Emma Plume Clifford, from Manderson, both on the Pine Ridge Reservation, began interviewing their tribesmen to record the continuing history of the Wounded Knee story.

In order to establish additional support and assistance for the project, we contacted Claudia Iron Hawk Sully, President of the Descendants of the Survivors of Wounded Knee. As the president of this organization, she was actively engaged in actions centered around the initial event and how it influences the Sioux people today. After reading the proposal for our project, she readily gave her assistance and support, and played an active and strong role. A resolution recognizing our relationship was approved by their tribal council, thus providing the second "tribal" acceptance of this project.

Several trips to Wounded Knee were necessary to coordinate aspects of this project. During each visit I was shocked to see that absolute despair and severe poverty still exists in pockets around the reservation. This disheartening discovery added more urgency and importance to this effort; for we hoped that this exhibition, and the true story it tells, would somehow make things easier for the people who suffered the most.

Compounding these conditions, the community seems to be divided into several opposing factions. As in other communities shackled by poverty, resources and funds are very scarce, and times are hard. When a bit of opportunity, in some form, does present itself, the various factions vie against each other to obtain that good fortune. Because the outside resources are so limited, only some factions are successful, creating resentment among the others. This is not an unusual predicament in communities with high unemployment (70% on some Indian reservations).

So far, the overall plan was working very well. The Sioux people were interviewing their own, with the taped interviews being transcribed locally, providing the interviewers, interviewees, and the transcribers with funding. These transcriptions would ultimately be given to Sioux colleges on the reservations, along with the recording equipment, when the project was complete. In this way, direct tribal benefit, although tiny, was assured. The following people were interviewed and their statements are a key part of this project: Daniel Afraid of Hawk, Matthew Zack Bear Shield, Tex Broken Nose, Mr. Chief Eagle, Alice Chief Eagle Weasel Bear, Bernice Eagle Hawk White Hawk, Steven Good Crow, Francis He Crow, Mike Her Many Horses, Clement C. High Hawk, Adolf Hollow Horn, Rachel Hollow Horn, Johnson Holy Rock, William Horn Cloud, Claudia Iron Hawk Sully, Lawson Iron Hawk, Phoebe Iron Hawk Red Elk, Emma Iron Plume Clifford, Calvin Jumping Bull, Jessie Kills Close to the Lodge Crow, Leonard Little Finger, Raymond Pipe on Head, Brother Simon, S.J., Nancy Weasel Bear Martin, Pearl White Dress, Eugenio White Hawk, Alex White Plume, and Severt Young Bear.

Ralph Moran, President, Rosebud Sioux Reservation; Charles W. Murphy, Chairman, Standing Rock Sioux Tribe; and Harold Salway,

President, Pine Ridge Reservation, on behalf of their tribes, endorsed and supported this project.

This third "Sioux" unit of the catalogue was ultimately organized in written form and woven together by another Sioux person, Ms. Jeanne Eder, a Ph.D. candidate born on the Fort Peck Indian Reservation. Her reputation and scholarly ability made this section come alive.

After talking with my Sioux friends who conducted the interviews, other Sioux people, and reading the transcripts, it became abundantly clear that they all intimately shared a passionate concern that can be summed up by a statement made by Ralph Moran, President of the Rosebud Sioux Tribe. The following statement is contained in their tribal endorsement supporting this project. He says: "I would hope that all references to *The Battle of Wounded Knee* be changed to *The Massacre at Wounded Knee* or to *The Tragedy at Wounded Knee*." Once it was apparent that the Sioux people share a desire for the truth to be known about the injustices at Wounded Knee, recognizing the action as a massacre became the primary goal of the exhibition. The art styles became secondary.

The final section of the project is the material itself. Research revealed a great number of beautiful Ghost Dance items from around the country, many either unpublished or not known or appreciated by the general public. Friends and acquaintances passed the word of our search, and numerous prospects surfaced from California to New York. Our goal was to include items that are spectacular, unknown and diverse; so in addition to the dresses, shirts, and leggings, we also included shields, a ball, a bustle, a quirt, and other objects, to show the incredible variety of the

4. *Shield, muslin, Sioux, c. 1890.*

objects. We realized that there would be a number of objects that would be too sensitive to show; those of a special religious nature or belonging to certain individuals. At no time did we see any garments that were blood-stained or perforated with bullet holes. These, of course, would have been immediately rejected.

Symbology

Ghost Dance symbology is interesting and there seems to be a relationship between it and other objects in the Indian culture. For example, the painting of dresses is very similar to the painting of a tipi. They are both large objects that allow room to paint diverse subjects and are laid out in the same way. The bottom third of the surface of the dresses and tipis usually represents the earth or, perhaps, yesterday—the known life. Here one can see jagged or wavy lines or even pyramids: these are mountains of the earth and are rendered in various hues and complexities. The top section is the sky or the heavens: here one sees crescents representing the moon, square crosses, Maltese crosses (representing stars), or

3. *Ball, Arapaho, c. 1900.*

the four or five point stars in the night sky, or even the round sun showing the day. They are all in the sky which, perhaps, represents tomorrow or another, better world. The central area of the painted tipi and the dress is today and portrays animals, praying pipes, people, corn—all either praying to or reaching for the sky. To me the symbology in many Ghost Dance dresses of this type shows the Indian people experiencing pain in the central area of today's world, while standing on the old earth and reaching for another world above—tomorrow.

As the religion spread, so did the proliferation of garments with the makers often using existing symbols, such as the eagle, buffalo, pyramids, Maltese crosses, square crosses, and even crescents. Each tribe may have added their own designs, using their symbolic representation of the Ghost Dance philosophy. So, when one sees any of these symbols on an item, it is not automatically of the Ghost Dance. They may have been painted at an earlier time, or more recently, since Ghost Dance materials command a higher price. Symbology and other aspects of the Ghost Dance are addressed in greater detail in the catalogue text.

Having intimate contact with the Indian people, and always the entrepreneur, Buffalo Bill Cody, in 1913, took part in organizing and filming a reenactment of the Wounded Knee massacre. As crude and insensitive as this concept was, the filming was monitored by General Miles and took place at the original site. In order to be as authentic as possible, Ghost Dance garments were made by the Sioux and many of these garments

6. *Dress, deerskin, Arapaho, c. 1885.*

5. *Rattle, Apache, c. 1890.*

still exist, offering an additional dilemma to the identification of real (1890) Ghost Dance materials.

Conclusion

To more fully understand the significance of Wounded Knee, one should know a bit about the native people involved. One must remember that most tribes can be divided into groups that share the same language stock. John Wesley Powell, director, U.S. Bureau of Ethnology in the late 1800s, classified Indian languages into 56 families. Using extended techniques Morris Swadesh in 1950, reduced the number to only five basic "phyla" or super language stocks. The Macro-Siouan phylum has several smaller divisions that include the Catawba, the Iroquoian,

7. *Dress, muslin, Arapaho, c. 1890 (?).*

Today, the Sioux Indian reservations are, in large part, occupied as follows:

Standing Rock — Hunkpapa and Sihasapa (Blackfeet)
Cheyenne River — Miniconjou and Sihasapa (Blackfeet)
Sisseton — Yanktons, Yanktonais
Crow Creek — Sichangu (Brules)
Lower Brule — Sichangu (Brules)
Pine Ridge — Oglala
Rosebud — Sichangu (Brules)

So, with this background, imagine a proud and noble people who have been here since the beginning. First, as residents of the Great Lakes area, they were pushed out onto the Plains, where they achieved their greatest glories. Then, once out on the flatlands, they were a formidable force, even as pedestrians. Being brave and strong, they

the Caddoan, and the Siouan. All of these tribes speak languages that can be related to each other.

In the Siouan Family there are the Crow, Hidatsa, Winnebago, Mandan, Iowa, Oto, Omaha, Osage, Ponca, Quapaw, Kansa, and Sioux (Dakota).

Understanding the Sioux component is more complex because, like Indian art, it is dynamic and changes over the years. First, no unit of the tribe can be identified solely by a single name. The word "Sioux" is a French corruption of the Chippewa word "Nadowe-is-iw" (the Lesser Adders), used by them to designate their ancient enemies. Royal Hassrick in his book *The Sioux* (University of Oklahoma Press, 1964), chose the term "Sioux" to refer to all subdivisions; we will do the same.

There were seven major divisions of the Sioux: 1. Oglala; 2. Sichangu (Brules); 3. Miniconjou; 4. Hunkpapa; 5. Sihasapa (Blackfeet); 6. Itazipcho (Sans Arcs); 7. Oohenonpa (Two Kettles). Linguistically their language can be differentiated into three parts: The *Lakota* dialect as spoken by the Tetons; *Nakota* as spoken by the Yankton, Yanktonai; and the *Dakota* as spoken by the Santee.

Around 1800 a new grouping took place. The Two Kettles, Sans Arcs, Blackfeet and Hunkpapa came together to be known by most as the Saones. The Oglala, Brules and Miniconjou became known as the Teton Sioux. With the introduction of the Reservation system it is unlikely that new groupings will emerge.

8. *Horned Bonnet, Northern Plains, c. 1840.*

9. *Karl Bodmer, (1809-1893). Noapeh an Assiniboin Indian, 1840-43.*

conquered enemies wherever they went. Armed with the gun by 1700 and obtaining the horse by 1750, their area of influence greatly increased and at one time they were a strong influence from Minnesota nearly to the Rocky Mountains in Montana and southward. Almost all tribes have their stories about battling the Sioux. The gesture that identifies them in sign language is the right flattened hand and fingers cutting the throat in a left to right movement.

They became some of the finest light cavalry horsemen in the world, and were called the Mighty Sioux. Suddenly, an unknown group of people from further east swept in and began conquering tribe after tribe with either disease, alcohol, treaties, deceit, military force, or all of these forces. One by one, the tribes fell until the Sioux were next. The invaders first put the Sioux people on the defensive by allying other tribes against them; then, by eliminating the buffalo as the main source of food, further weakened them. After a series of such activities, the Western Sioux signed the Fort Laramie treaty in 1868. The treaty designated the Sioux lands as all of South Dakota, large parts of Wyoming, North Dakota, Montana and Nebraska, but limited their freedom. Utilizing the same pressures, the reservations were further eroded and the Sioux people fought against this action man-to-man, hand-to-hand; but the whites were as many as the blades of grass and their weapons and technology were overwhelming. So, suddenly, within a short period of time, these lords of the Plains were unhorsed and restricted to reservations with their lifeUs blood, the buffalo, eliminated. The rations guaranteed to them by treaty were threatened if they did not obey the usually corrupt Indian agents, and they suffered like never before.

The Sioux people must have prayed to The Spirit Above or even questioned the Christian priests and asked, "Why is this happening to us? We have done nothing wrong, but our world is ending." They did Sun Dances. They went into the sweat lodge, they sacrificed; but still, this evil followed them and the new diseases killed. Suddenly, a message came from the West that promised good things, a return to the old life style. So they desperately danced the Ghost Dance in a final effort to survive, once again praying. But the newcomers would have none of it, and their dreams were shattered on the killing field of Wounded Knee where tribal accounts say over 400 of them perished. And, as a final outrage, the U.S. government awarded eighteen Congressional Medals of Honor to the soldiers who killed them. Buffalo, land, spirit, prayer, all the basic fundamentals of life were lost—taken by the

10. *Saddle Blanket, Northern Plains, c. 1840.*

Indian Land Loss

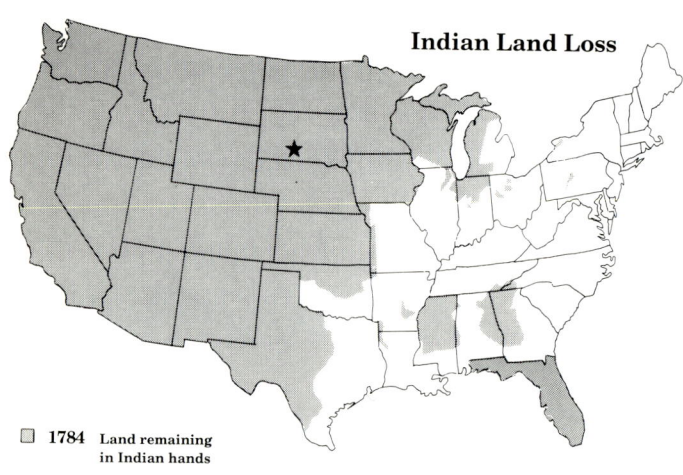

1784 Land remaining in Indian hands

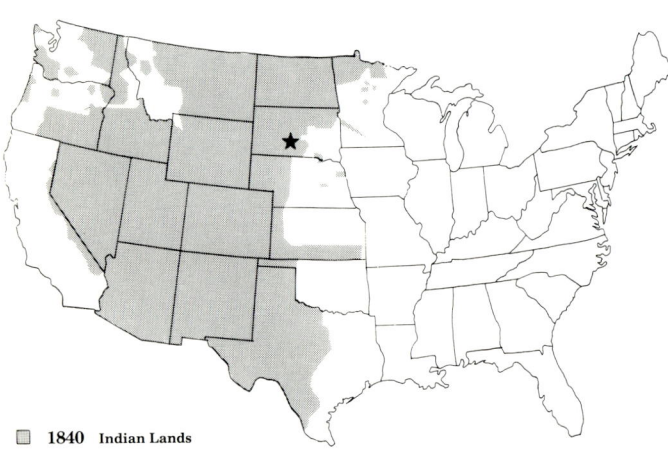

1840 Indian Lands

Reservations Today
South Dakota
Standing Rock
Sisseton
Cheyenne River
Pierre
Crow Creek
Rapid City
Lower Brule
Sioux Falls
Pine Ridge
Rosebud
Yankton

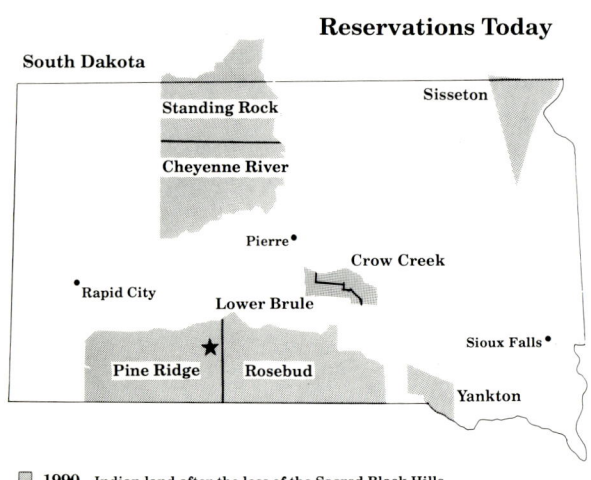

1990 Indian land after the loss of the Sacred Black Hills and other lands.

★ *Wounded Knee.*

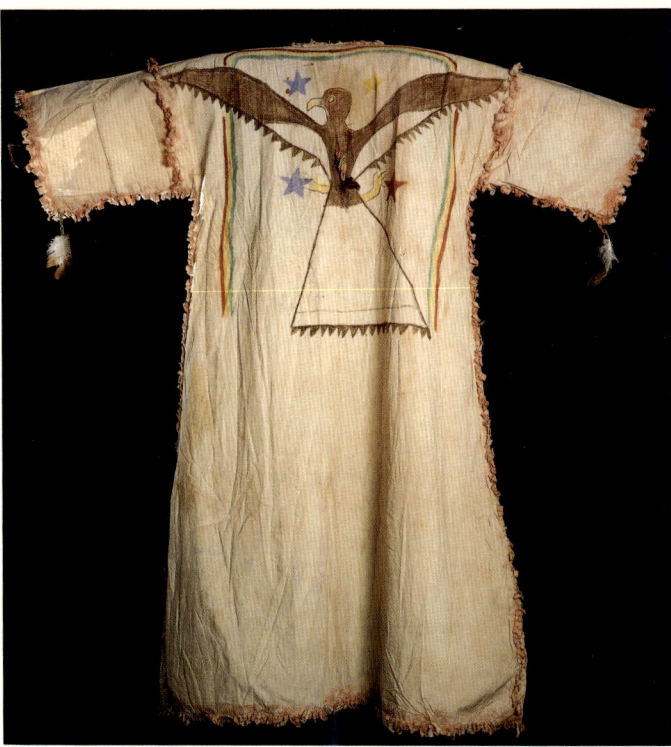

11. *Dress, muslin, Sioux, c. 1890.*

wa'sicu—white man. What was left? Not even human dignity.

In reviewing the conditions that led up to Wounded Knee, some startling discoveries can be detected. When the non-Indians surrounded Indian country over 100 years ago, they were not content to take most of the Sioux lands, even their sacred Black Hills, they wanted more, they wanted everything, they wanted everything that made the Sioux what they were: religion, art, philosophy—everything. Unable to sit quietly for this genocide, some of the tribe resisted, many by adopting the new religion that promised a return to the old, pre-white man days. This religion alarmed many non-Indians, both locally and nationally; and, spurred on by the inflammatory and inaccurate news headlines, the U.S. government forces reacting only to the wail of a small segment of the population, swept in, assasinated the Sioux leaders and killed the religion.

The frightening aspect of the historic scenario is that the conditions that created Wounded Knee are still with the tribes today—they have always existed. For the most part, Indians still are poverty-stricken, held in place by the forces of racism. They are surrounded by non-Indians still seeking their few remaining acres of land, their water, their religion and all the rest. The newspapers are there too, ready to exaggerate conditions so they can sell more issues. And the U.S. government has been augmented by state governments who, rather than objectively seeking justice, still back the issues that will provide them the most votes so they can stay in power. The evil sore that is Wounded Knee will not go away. It erupted again in 1973 with Wounded Knee II, when the Indians seized the trading post at Wounded Knee, to once again proclaim their outrage at the way they have been, and are being, treated. Basically, very little has changed since 1890; all of the conditions are still with us for another "Wounded Knee" and we have to live in this world.

As Mike Her Many Horses, Tribal Councilman from the Wounded Knee district, says:

The visitors traveling to Wounded Knee, South Dakota, to view the 1890 Massacre Site usually ask, "Is this all there is to it?" Only a simple stone marker tells the story of this mass murder and tragedy. A marker erected by the Horn Cloud family, survivors of that massacre. A white flag representing the truce which was in place when Big Foot's band was escorted to Wounded Knee now has flown for four years, put in place by the Big Foot Memorial Riders to remind the public of the events that took place under Big Foot's white flag of truce. The simple truth of Wounded Knee is that it was mass murder under a flag of truce. No apology, no compensation for the survivors or their heirs has ever been forthcoming from the U.S. government. It is as if the event never took place at all and we don't exist. Wounded Knee remains an open festering chapter of American history. Indian people of the Cheyenne River, Rosebud and Pine Ridge reservations have kept the book on Wounded Knee open. Open for the American conscience to deal with if they can.

Somehow in order for the world to be normal again, these grievances must be addressed and satisfied. The Sioux people proposed legislation to Congress on the 25th of September, 1990. They seek only three things: compensation for the damages sustained by their people at Wounded Knee, 1890, a monument to be built for their ancestors who died there, and an apology from the United States Government for the massacre of their ancestors a hundred years ago. Imagine, is that too much to ask?

When these simple requests are finally met perhaps their sacred hoop will once again be whole.

George P. Horse Capture
Cody, Wyoming 1990

12. *Entrance to Mass Burial Grave, Wounded Knee Cemetery.*

13. *Pennant, company guidon.*

WOUNDED KNEE: A HISTORY
by
Alvin M. Josephy, Jr.

December 28, 1890. A gentle wind, unusually mild for that time of year, blew across the South Dakota hills. Near Porcupine Butte on the Pine Ridge Indian reservation, a band of Miniconjou Sioux—120 men and 230 women and children, many on ponies, others in horsedrawn wagons or walking beside their travois—topped a ridge and started down its slope. Ahead of them, two miles distant on the lower ground, a long skirmish line of dismounted troopers of the 7th Cavalry, Custer's old regiment, waited for them. In the center of the bluecoats' line, two Hotchkiss guns pointed directly at the oncoming Indians.

The Sioux were tired from traveling and hungry. They had come from their home village on another reservation more than 150 miles to the north, hurrying across the plains and through the Badlands, evading other bluecoat armies to seek safety among the Oglala Sioux who had invited them to Pine Ridge. The Miniconjous did not want to fight. Their chief, Big Foot, known among the Sioux as a man of peace and a leader of wisdom and mild manner, lay dying of pneumonia in one of the wagons, bundled like a mummy in a blanket, an old overcoat, and a scarf, and dripping blood from his nose. A white flag fluttered from a pole attached to his lurching wagon.

No one knew if the soldiers would let them pass. Now that the Miniconjous had reached the Pine Ridge reservation, there was nowhere to go but straight ahead toward the agency where they would meet the Oglalas. The women and children were frightened, and the men were uneasy. But the warriors were determined to defend the people. Instinctively, the young men turned their horses' heads and spread out to right and left, forming a protective battle line opposite the cavalrymen.

The Indians came to a halt, and several Sioux went forward on foot to ask the cavalry commander, Major Samuel M. Whitside, for a parley. He refused to talk to them and demanded to see Big Foot. The chief's wagon moved up to the line of bluecoats, and Whitside leaned over, saw that the Indian leader was sick, and reached down and shook his hand. Turning aside, the officer conversed with his head scout. He wanted to disarm the Indians and take their horses from them, but the scout persuaded him that it would be unsafe to try to do it here. Women and children would be killed resisting, and the warriors would get away. Better, first, bring them into camp.

Through an interpreter, Whitside told Big Foot that he must take his people to the cavalrymen's camp on Wounded Knee Creek, about eight miles away, on the road to the agency. It is not known how much the sick Miniconjou chief understood, but he said, all right, that was where he was going anyway. The officer also asked Big Foot to surrender, and the chief, according to the commander, agreed to do so.

The Sioux were relieved. There would be no fighting. As word of Big Foot's surrender circulated among the soldiers, they, too, felt better. Some of them became friendly to the Indians, and Whitside had Big Foot transferred from his springless wagon to a more comfortable Army ambulance. Together, the Sioux and the troopers made their way across the hills to the cavalrymen's camp on Wounded Knee Creek.

By noon the next day, it was over. Big Foot and almost 250 of his people were dead, scattered across the frozen ground at Wounded Knee. More than 50 other Indians, some of whom would die later, were wounded, and uncounted others who had got away from the campsite were believed to have died or been wounded. Twenty-five cavalrymen were also dead, and 37 soldiers and two civilians (a priest and a halfbreed interpreter) had been wounded. In the whirlwind, a legacy of confusion, hatred, and mistrust was let loose to haunt a century of relations between the Sioux and the American government. In the Indians'

14. *U.S. Army Soldier dressed for winter on the Plains, c. 1890.*

mind, December 29, 1890, the date of the horrendous killing of the Miniconjous' old people and warriors, of their wives and babies, was established as a day of infamy.

What had happened on that terrible morning following the day when Whitside had intercepted the Sioux? What had Big Foot and his people done that brought them to such a sudden and violent end? To get at the answers to those questions, one must look back in history and contemplate the events of the preceding 40 years—the misjudgments, the misunderstandings, the aggressions, and the deceits—that led, almost inexorably, to the appointment at Wounded Knee.

Forty years before, in 1850, the various Sioux tribes, living and hunting on a great part of the northern prairies and plains from Minnesota and Iowa to what are now Montana and Wyoming, were still unconquered and free. By and large, they lived in harmony and balance with all else in their universe, possessing every right that freedom implies. They were free to govern themselves, to conduct their lives, social relations, and economies as they wished, to maintain their cultural values and traditions, and to believe in and practice their own religion.

Already, however, the Sioux were beginning to clash with whites who were invading their country. Emigrants, miners, teamsters, and others, bound for Oregon or California, were crossing their lands in growing numbers, slaying the buffalo and other game on which the Sioux depended, disrupting tribal life, and leaving in their wake dreaded sicknesses that killed the Indian people.

To safeguard the travelers from attempts by the concerned Indians to halt the white men's incursions, the government in 1851 called many of the plains tribes, including members of the Western, or Teton, branch of the Sioux, to a council at Fort Laramie and induced them to permit the use of roads through their lands, as well as the building of military posts to protect the roads. In return for the Indians' agreement not to interfere with white traffic on such highways as the Oregon Trail, the government promised the tribes the payment of annuities and the recognition of their ownership of the territory that each one claimed as its own.

Although the treaty at first was observed conscientiously by the Sioux, aggressive acts against them by intolerant and racist whites who used the Oregon Trail kept tensions high. In 1854, a misunderstanding over the Indians possession of an emigrant's cow and an impulsive attack on a Sioux village by a hot-headed army officer exploded in hostilities, marked the next year by a savage assault by the Army on an unsuspecting Brule Sioux camp and an invading march by a military expedition through the Sioux country from Fort Laramie to the Missouri River in an attempt to overawe the Indians. Although quiet returned, the Sioux realized that their lands and freedom were no longer safe.

Events soon confirmed their fears. In 1851 and 1858, the Eastern Sioux in Minnesota, pressed by settlers who wanted their lands, and threatened and deceived by corrupt traders, agents, and government negotiators, were forced to cede almost all of their territory to the whites. Starving, lied to, and filled with grievances and frustrations, the desperate Eastern Sioux tribes in 1862 rose up and killed some 350 Minnesota settlers. The sensational outburst was quickly put down by the Army, which captured many of the Indians, hanged 38 of them, and pursued others westward across the northern plains, where some of them found shelter with groups of Hanktonai and Teton Sioux. The Army took the war to these tribes, falling on camps of innocent, buffalo-hunting bands of Yanktonais, as well as Hunkpapa, Miniconjou, and other Teton Sioux, and spreading the conflict to the west side of the Missouri River.

The hostilities on the northern plains soon merged with renewed fighting farther south along the Oregon Trail. Trying to protect supply and communication routes across the central plains during the Civil War, the Army attempted to clear the Brule and Oglala Sioux entirely out of the Platte River Valley, which the Oregon Trail followed. Along with Cheyennes and Arapahos, who were being forced out of their own hunting grounds in Colorado and Kansas (and some of whose people were treacherously attacked and massacred by Colorado volunteers at Sand Creek in 1864), the Brules and Oglalas fought back, thwarting plans to push them off land which the government in the Treaty of 1851 had recognized as belonging to them.

The fighting along the Platte was the start of a series of defensive wars waged by the seven different Teton Sioux tribes to retain their country. Gold was discovered in western Montana, and even before the end of the Civil War, prospectors, supported by the Army, began traveling through Sioux territory, blazing trails to the western mines. In 1865, an unsuccessful military campaign through the heart of the Indians' powder River hunting grounds, and treaties made with a few compliant bands along the Missouri River, failed to halt Sioux resistance to the new incursions. During the next two years, persistent attacks by Sioux warriors under the Oglala chief, Red Cloud, forced the Army to abandon its attempts to protect the Bozeman Trail, a principal route that ran from the Oregon Trail through the Powder River hunting grounds to the northwestern gold fields.

To the Sioux, a treaty signed with the government at Fort Laramie in 1868 appeared to acknowledge a total Indian victory, for, according to their understanding, it promised to bar troops and other whites from their country, let the Indians live in peace, and allow them to trade at posts along the Platte River. But there were other provisions, and the Indians later insisted that the whites did not tell them truthfully all that was in the treaty.

For one thing, the Sioux, in signing the document, relinquished their right to much of the land that had been recognized as theirs by the Treaty of 1851, retaining only the territory of the present state of South Dakota west of the Missouri River. That area was designated as a Great Sioux Reservation, and the treaty called for all the Western Sioux to move onto it and, under the supervision and authority of agents, to accept individual family allotments and settle down to become farmers like white men. Any future cession of reservation land, it was noted, would have to be approved by three-fourths of all the adult male Indians. At the same time, another provision, somewhat confusedly, reserved the right of the Indians to continue to hunt on lands they had relinquished outside of the new reservation where they had traditionally hunted.

Although the Sioux did not realize it, the potential now existed for the government to limit severely not only the tribes" ownership and use of land, but also their freedom. The formal existence of a reservation, onto which the Indians would have to move, set the stage for control of them by agents and troops and for their enforced "civilizing" and assimilation by missionaries and teachers.

Signs of what lay ahead became evident almost immediately. Still determined to clear the Indians out of the Platte Valley, where the transcontinental railroad was now being built, the government soon after the signing of the treaty prohibited the Indians from trading at posts along the Platte River and ordered them to report to agencies on the new reservation. The resulting turmoil caused a split among the Sioux. The more peacefully-inclined Oglalas and Brules, following Chiefs Red Cloud and Spotted Tail, were tired of fighting and settled down at the agencies. At first, as a concession to the chiefs, who claimed they had been lied to at the Fort Laramie Treaty meeting, the agencies were located outside the reservation boundaries, giving the chiefs the ability to trade at the Platte River posts and thus the illusion that they still possessed the freedom of movement. But, very shortly, those Indians and their agencies were moved to sites inside the reservation. The other Oglalas and Brules, as well as the Yanktonai and the other five Teton tribes—the Miniconjous, Hunkpapas, Sans Arcs, Two Kettles, and Blackfeet Sioux—stayed north of the Platte River to avoid the whites and ignoring the agencies, continued in freedom to follow their old hunting life.

Peace was short-lived. In a flagrant violation of the 1868 Treaty, an expedition led by Lieutenant Colonel George A. Custer invaded the Sioux reservation in 1874 and discovered gold in the Black Hills, the most sacred part of the tribes' lands. A stampede followed, and neither the Indians nor troops could stem the torrent of whites who entered the reservation. To try to avoid hostilities, the government offered to buy the Black Hills from the Sioux. The Indians, largely under the influence of the non-agency hunting bands, whom the whites called "hostiles," refused to bargain away the Hills, and in November 1875, the frustrated Grant Administration, to get the "hostiles" under control, ordered them to come in to the agencies by January 31, 1876, or be driven in by the Army.

The hunting bands, led by such chiefs as Crazy Horse (Oglala) and Sitting Bull (Hunkpapa), either could not or would not come in on such short notice in mid-winter, and in March troops started after them. The campaign to round up the Sioux reached a climax on June 25, 1876, when the Indians killed Custer and more than 250 members of his 7th Cavalry who had rashly attacked a huge concentration of their bands at the Little Bighorn River in Montana. Thereafter, as the bands split up, punitive military expeditions pursued them through the fall and winter. Sitting Bull and many of his followers escaped to Canada, where the Hunkpapa chief, who was also the spiritual leader of his people, remained in exile until 1881. After his return to the United States, he was confined at Fort Randall, and in 1883 was permitted to rejoin his followers at the Standing Rock agency on the Sioux reservation.

Given little time by the pursuing troops to hunt or rest, the other bands were beset by hunger, cold, and sickness. Time and again, they had to fight off soldiers who overtook them. Eventually, one by one, the bands gave themselves up at the agencies. The last to surrender were Crazy Horse and his Oglalas who, though starving, rode proudly into Fort Robinson near the Red Cloud agency in May, 1877. Four months later, suspected of planning to escape and regain his freedom, Crazy Horse was murdered in a scuffle in the guard room at the fort. With his death passed one of the greatest war chiefs and patriots of the Sioux Nation.

The fortunes of all the Western Sioux, meanwhile, had deteriorated rapidly. They had lost their freedom, and also the Black Hills. Ignoring the provision of the 1868 Treaty that said that no new cession of Sioux land could be made without the approval of three-fourths of the adult Sioux males, government commissioners in 1877 bullied the "non-hostile" peace chiefs at the agencies into signing a new agreement, which once again was not fully described to them. Threatened with the loss of their rations or with exile to the Indian Territory (today's Oklahoma) if they refused to sign, the chiefs, in the absence of the "hostile" bands that were then fighting the soldiers, gave away the Black Hills and a large part of the western side of the reservation.

With the Sioux beaten militarily and reduced to the status of captives, the government's policy toward them became one of hastening their assimilation by destroying their culture and the age-old structures of their society. The bands settled down at different sites on the Great Sioux Reservation, still looking for guidance from their chiefs and spiritual leaders. White agents, often corrupt and incompetent, as well as missionaries and teachers—all of them supported by the nearby presence of troops ready to enforce their orders—held complete power over the Indians, asserting their authority by punishments and threats of punishment, including the withholding of food, imprisonment, or banishment to the Indian Territory.

Without freedom of movement, the peoples' old routines of daily life became a memory of the past. The young men could no longer make war or hunt buffalo, and idleness and dependency on government rations sapped their morale and self-respect. The rations themselves were usually so meager and of such poor quality that malnutrition, sickness, and even starvation were common. The agents tried to teach the Sioux men to farm—considered women's work by the plains tribes—and some attempted to raise crops. Grasshoppers, drought, hail, and inexperience all conspired against them, however, and the results were slim and frustrating.

At the same time, the agents, following orders from Washington, did everything possible to undermine the traditional organization of the tribes and the influence of the chiefs and medicine men. Indian police forces, appointed by the agents, competed with the chiefs for authority and acquired much of the power exercised formerly by special Sioux societies, which lost their reasons for existence and withered away. Ignoring and humiliating the chiefs, the agents chose lesser men with whom to deal, forcing the Indians to look to the new appointees to protect their interests. As the peoples' ties with the old chiefs weakened, the agents encouraged them also to move away from their chiefs' camps and spread out over the reservation as independent families.

Meanwhile, Sioux cultural and spiritual beliefs and practices were attacked as barbaric and pagan. In an assault on the Indians' freedom of religion, ceremonies and sacred rituals like those of the Sun Dance were prohibited. The practices of medicine men, both medical and spiritual, were banned, and Sioux holy men who defied the ban were arrested. The singing of Sioux songs, the telling of Sioux legends and lore to the young, the perpetuation of all manifestations of Sioux culture were discouraged, and Sioux children were taken from their families, often forcibly, and sent away to distant boarding schools to be taught to be like whites.

The harsh years of enforced assimilation demoralized and again divided the Sioux. Some, seeing no alternative, decided to try to follow the white men's road as the only path offering hope for the future. Cooperating with the agents and missionaries, sending their children to school and accepting Christianity, they became known as progressives. The others, still clinging to their traditional beliefs and customs, had as little as possible to do with the agents, who watched them suspiciously and regarded them as nonprogressives and potentially dangerous.

In the 1880s, new tensions arose that brought the two groups together temporarily in common defense of the reservation against the whites. Settlers and real estate developers in eastern South Dakota, demanding that the Sioux give up more of their land, were joined by politicians and investment interests in the East who pointed out that the Great Sioux Reservation, which extended solidly from the northern to the southern border of South Dakota, cut off the Black Hills from the rest of the Territory and barred the building of a railroad west of the Missouri River. Washington supported the new assault on the Indians' lands, and in 1883 a government commission went west to try to talk the Sioux into ceding about half of the reservation and agree to the breaking up of the rest of it into a number of separate reservations that would geographically divide the different Lakota-speaking Teton tribes from each other. The commissioners returned to Washington, claiming that they had won the Indians' approval, but the Sioux, supported by Indian rights organizations in the East, contested the claim as fraudulent. It was then discovered that the commissioners had induced fewer than 400 Sioux—rather than the three-fourths of all adult males required under the still-applicable Treaty of 1868—to sign the agreement, and when another attempt to gather enough signatures failed, Congress dropped the matter.

The passage of the Dawes Allotment Act in 1887, however, provided a new opportunity to those who coveted the Sioux lands. Under the Act, reservations were to be broken up and the assimilation of Indians hastened by allotting the Indians separate parcels of land which they and their families would own and be able to farm like white men. After all the allotments had been made, the surplus land would be thrown open to white settlers under the Homestead laws. Making use of the Dawes Act, special legislation was framed to achieve the goals that had been sought unsuccessfully in 1883 with regard to the Sioux reservation. However, the legislation reversed the order of procedure called for by the Dawes Act. Instead of first making the allotments to the Indians and then selling to whites what was left over, it directed that negotiations be conducted first with the Indians for "surplus" land, which it was estimated would total some nine million acres.

The Sioux no longer trusted the government, and when negotiators appeared at the agencies, many progressives stood firmly with the non-progressives and refused to sign the agreement. In 1889, however, another group of commissioners, headed by Major General George Crook, promised the Sioux more money and many benefits and finally wore the Indians down. Crook's commission won enough signatures from the progressive Indians to satisfy Congress that three-fourths of the adult males had approved the land agreement. Approximately half of the Great Sioux Reservation was then opened to white settlement, and on the unceded land, six separate reservations—Standing Rock, Cheyenne River, Crow Creek, Lower Brule, Rosebud, and Pine Ridge—were created for the Teton Sioux tribes and the Yanktonai.

The new loss of land infuriated many of the non-progressive Indians, who blamed the progressives for caving in to the whites. But more blows were to come. Two weeks after the commissioners left South Dakota, orders were received cutting down the Indians' rations drastically. The reduction had nothing to do with the land agreement— a Congressional economy move had cut the Sioux appropriation for the fiscal year 1890—but the

Indians, already close to starvation, regarded it as another betrayal. The government had gotten the land, and now it would let the Indians die of hunger. Already under attack, the progressives suffered other embarrassments. General Crook died in March, 1890, and none of the benefits he had promised the Indians ever came through. Also in March, reservation land designated as surplus,

15. *Shirt, deerskin, Pawnee, c. 1890.*

and therefore ceded, was thrown open to whites without giving Indians who lived there a chance to claim allotments on it. The confusion caused by the arbitrary action added to the Indians' resentments.

The winter of 1889-90 was a hard one for the Sioux. In addition to hunger, depression over the continued betrayals and loss of land, as well as despair and general hopelessness about the future, the Indians were battered by epidemics of whooping cough, measles, and influenza that took many lives. As spring approached, there seemed to be no end to their misery, no way out of their travail.

In March, in the depths of their despondency, the people were stirred by exciting news. During the previous fall, rumors had reached many of the western tribes, including the Sioux, about an Indian Messiah who had appeared in Nevada, working miracles and preaching of the coming of a new world without whites, where the Indians would be happy and free again. In their adversity, some of the Sioux had grasped at the story and had sent a delegation of eleven emissaries from Pine Ridge, Rosebud, and Cheyenne River to Nevada to look into it. Returning in March, the emissaries reported that the rumors were true.

A Northern Paiute sheepherder and shaman named Wovoka on the Walker River reservation had fallen ill, it appeared, and during the solar eclipse had had a vision in which he was transported to heaven. There, God had shown him a radiant world where there were no whites and where all the dead Indians and the former huge herds of buffalo and wild game were still alive. This happy world, Wovoka was told, was already coming through the heavens from the west toward America. By adopting certain prayers and practices, the Indians still on earth would be lifted in the air as the new world met and rolled over the present one, obliterating it and driving the white men back across the ocean to where they had come from. The Indians would then be lowered to an eternal life of abundance and peace among their returned ancestors, relatives, and friends in the new world. Charged with conveying to the Indians what he had seen and been told, Wovoka after his vision had returned to earth as a Messiah who would rescue the tribes from their despair and suffering.

The religion he preached was a pacifistic one, based in large part on tenets of Christianity. To deserve the new world, which was to arrive in the spring of 1891, his Indian audiences were admonished not to fight among themselves or

16. *Bustle, Arapaho, c. 1885.*

with white men, but to be honest, peaceful, and chaste and to follow a moralistic code of conduct closely resembling that of the Biblical Ten Commandments. Specifically, Wovoka taught the Indians prayers, songs, and a special dance they were to perform at certain intervals that would enable them to receive advance glimpses of the wonderful new world that was approaching. To convince his visitors, like the Sioux, that he was, indeed, a Messiah speaking the truth, he used his shamanistic powers and knowledge to perform deeds that appeared to be miracles.

Initially, most of the Sioux people were skeptical of the reports of the new religion that their emissaries brought back to them. But the hardships of the winter continued into the summer of 1890, and new threats arose to increase their anxiety. First of all, a severe drought struck South Dakota, drying up the Indians' crops. At the same time, census-takers decided that the government was supplying more rations than there were Sioux, and the rations were cut again.

Starvation and sickness increased, and the death toll of the people, particularly of babies, children, and elders, rose. In the Indians' desperation, quarrels broke out about boundaries and living sites on the new reservations. And, finally, troops began to appear on the borders of the reservations, bringing unease and fear to the tribes that were now separated from each other. One group of cavalrymen, arriving to keep an eye on the Indians at Pine Ridge, established a camp just outside the western boundary of that reservation. Other soldiers, ordered to protect whites who were settling on the newly-ceded land, based themselves on the Cheyenne River, threateningly close to the reservation of that name and also to a band of non-progressive Miniconjous led by Chief Big Foot who had vigorously opposed the land agreement in 1889.

During the summer, a 41-year-old medicine man of Big Foot's band named Kicking Bear visited the Arapaho Indians in Wyoming, who had adopted Wovoka's religion and were zealously conducting the dance that he had prescribed to his followers. An Oglala from Pine Ridge who had married a Miniconjou and joined her band, Kicking Bear had been one of the Sioux emissaries to Nevada and, with his brother-in-law, Short Bull, a Brule from Rosebud, had become an ardent disciple of the Messiah. Observing the Arapahos, Kicking Bear acquired further information on how to conduct the dance of the new religion.

Garbed in loose-fitting Ghost Shirts, painted with stars, crescents, birds, and other symbols of the religion, and believed to make the wearers invulnerable to bullets, the Arapahos clasped hands and danced sideways in a great circle, singing for the return of the dead Indians and the buffalo. The dancers began slowly. Then the tempo increased. Individuals danced by themselves, praying, falling in a trance, and receiving visions in which they saw the happy land described by the Messiah.

Returning to the Sioux in August with what he had learned from the Arapahos, Kicking Bear stopped at Pine Ridge and found many of the distraught Oglalas now eager to adopt the new religion. Following Kicking Bear's instructions, dance groups were formed on different parts of the reservation, and numerous Oglalas were soon holding dances from morning till night. Their

17. *Dress, deerskin, Southern Plains, c. 1890 (?).*

enthusiasm was contagious and, like a prairie fire, the religion spread to the Rosebud reservation, where Short Bull organized Brule dance groups, and then to Cheyenne River, where Kicking Bear showed the members of Big Foot's band and others how to conduct the dances. In October, Sitting Bull invited Kicking Bear to bring information about the new religion to the Standing Rock reservation. The great Hunkpapa chief, living among his followers in a camp on Grand River, had been a thorn in the side of Standing Rock's dictatorial agent, James McLaughlin, ever since he had been allowed to live on the reservation in 1883, following his return from Canada and confinement at Fort Randall. Determined to destroy the chief's prestige and influence, agent McLaughlin was delighted when the government permitted the chief to leave the reservation and go on tour with the Wild West show of William F. "Buffalo Bill" Cody. McLaughlin wished it would rid him of the chief forever, but when the tour ended, Sitting Bull returned to his followers on Grand River on the reservation and revived his feud with the agent.

Sitting Bull had his doubts about the new religion of Wovoka, but under Kicking Bear's tutelage, his followers took it up and began to dance. Soon McLaughlin heard about it, and had the Indian police eject Kicking Bear from the reservation. The ousting played into the hands of Sitting Bull, who whether or not he believed in Wovoka's teachings, took over the leadership of the new religion on Standing Rock. As the dances continued to gain adherents, McLaughlin threatened Sitting Bull, but to no avail. Finally, the agent asked his superiors in the Interior Department to order the confinement of the defiant chief in a military prison. In the East, Sitting Bull was too famous an Indian, however, and, afraid of public criticism, the Secretary of the Interior hesitated to initiate such a drastic action.

In the meantime, the anti-white aspects and the highly emotional dances of the new religion alarmed the agents at Pine Ridge, Rosebud, and Cheyenne River and spread fear among the non-Indian populations of North and South Dakota and Nebraska who adjoined the reservations. Few whites could comprehend the essentially non-violent nature of the Indians' movement, which was becoming known awesomely as the Ghost Dance, and most were sure that it was the ominous prelude to a Sioux uprising. Newly-appointed to their jobs by the incoming administration of President Benjamin Harrison and largely unknowledgeable in dealing with Indians, the agents tried unsuccessfully to halt the dancing. As the Sioux flaunted their defiance, and the dancing continued, the agents, as well as newspaper editors and fearful business and political leaders in the white communities in the region, appealed to Washington to send troops onto the reservations to control the Indians.

On October 31, President Harrison, through the War Department, ordered Brigadier General Thomas H. Ruger, commanding the Department of Dakota, to investigate the situation. At Standing Rock, Ruger met with agent McLaughlin and, agreeing that the Ghost Dance would collapse there if Sitting Bull were removed from the reservation, laid plans to have the agency's Indian police force, supported by troops from nearby Fort Yates, arrest the chief. At Cheyenne River, Ruger found conditions less threatening, but ordered reinforcements sent to Fort Bennett, near the reservation's agency.

Meanwhile, the inexperienced agent at Pine Ridge had increasing difficulties with the Ghost Dancers on his reservation and finally panicked after a near-violent confrontation with some 200 of them who defied his authority. "Indians are dancing in the snow and are wild and crazy," he wired the Commissioner of Indian Affairs in Washington. "We need protection and we need it now."

The Secretary of the Interior agreed at last to ask the President and the War Department for assistance, and on November 17, many elements of the U.S. Army began heading for the Sioux reservations to overawe and suppress the Ghost Dancers. By order of Major General Nelson A. Miles, commander of the military Division of Missouri, 170 members of the 9th Cavalry Regiment and 200 infantrymen of the 2d and 8th Regiments, with a Hotchkiss cannon and a Gatling gun, arrived on the Pine Ridge reservation on November 20 and established a tent camp at the agency. On the same day, 230 members of the 9th Cavalry and the 8th Infantry, with another Hotchkiss cannon, reached the Rosebud agency. The following week saw the arrival of more troops: four additional companies of the 2d Infantry, another troop of the 9th Cavalry, the entire 7th Cavalry, which Custer had once commanded, and a battery of the 1st Artillery all joined the huge camp at Pine Ridge. At Rosebud, four companies of the 21st Infantry reinforced the troops already there. In addition, Miles ordered units in New Mexico, Kansas, and Montana to the two reservations and authorized the enlistment of two troops of Indian scouts from among the mixed-breed and progressive Sioux at Pine Ridge. The entire force was placed under the command of Brigadier General John R. Brooke, who came to

18. *Seventh Cavalry, Wounded Knee, c. 1890.*

Pine Ridge from Omaha, where he commanded the Department of the Platte.

The overwhelming show of power—more than 1,000 soldiers occupied the tent city at Pine Ridge—was intended to provide protection to the agencies and to the "loyal" or "friendly" Indians. In addition, the troops' arrival had another impact. Fearful of being attacked by the soldiers, many Sioux abandoned the dance groups and, obeying General Brooke's directions, moved into the agencies to join the progressives and establish tipi villages near the troops' camps.

The first reaction of the more dedicated Oglala and Brule Ghost Dancers on both Pine Ridge and Rosebud was one of anger. Uniting into a single camp of some 500 lodges, they moved with Short Bull, Kicking Bear, and other chiefs into the rugged Badlands in the northwestern corner of the Pine Ridge reservation and, taking refuge on a plateau in a natural fortress known as the Stronghold, continued their dancing. During the following days, General Brooke sent a stream of emissaries to them—progressives, halfbreeds, and a well-liked priest from the Holy Rosary Mission at Pine Ridge—promising them food and other inducements if they would stop dancing and come in to the Pine Ridge agency. At first, the dancers resisted the emissaries' pleas, reminding them of the Indians' many grievances against the whites and complaining that the Army was now trying to stop the peaceful practice of their religion. The holdouts' resolve gradually weakened, however, and, suffering from hunger and cold, many of the chiefs and their followers began to leave the Stronghold and head back to the agency. By mid-December, only the militant Short Bull, Kicking Bear, and some 200 other diehards were left in the Badlands, fighting off occasional attacks by groups of local militia and cowboys, but continuing to dance.

On the Standing Rock reservation farther north, McLaughlin, meanwhile, was delaying the arrest of Sitting Bull until the arrival of freezing weather and snow when he believed the Hunkpapas would be less inclined to leave their cabins and risk a war in defense of their chief. While McLaughlin waited, General Miles, who had no use for the civilian agents on the reservations and felt that the Army should be in charge of the Indians, took matters into his own hands. Convinced that Sitting Bull was responsible for the entire Ghost Dance problem and that his removal would go far toward ending the threat to the whites, he hit on the idea of having the chief's former employer, Buffalo Bill Cody, talk him into surrendering. Armed with an order for the arrest of Sitting Bull, Cody arrived at Standing Rock, only to be thwarted by McLaughlin. Resenting the interference by the showman, McLaughlin complained by wire to the Secretary of the Interior, who had the President telegraph orders back to the reservation suspending Cody's assignment. The former scout left Standing Rock, feeling confused and victimized.

Despite the rebuff over Buffalo Bill, Miles still held the upper hand. Shortly after Cody's departure, McLaughlin was instructed by Washington not to arrest any Indian without orders from the Secretary of the Interior or the military—meaning Miles. On December 10, with his authority made clear, Miles moved again. Persuaded that the situation on the reservations was growing more dangerous, that Sitting Bull was trying to unite all the tribes of the northern plains in an uprising, and that he should be arrested at once, he ordered Lieutenant Colonel William F. Drum, the commanding officer of Fort Yates near the Standing Rock agency, to seize the chief.

Drum had already been cooperating with McLaughlin in forming a plan for the chief's arrest, and they now prepared to put it into effect. The date set for the arrest was pushed forward when McLaughlin learned that Kicking Bear and Short Bull had invited Sitting Bull to visit the Brule and Oglala Ghost Dancers at the Stronghold on the Pine Ridge reservation. The prospect of the influential chief joining forces with the defiant Sioux at the Stronghold alarmed McLaughlin and Drum, and they determined to seize Sitting Bull before he could leave Standing Rock.

In the early morning hours of December 15, the agent sent a force of some 40 Indian policemen through a cold, drizzling rain to Sitting Bull's camp on Grand River. Behind them, two troops of the 8th Cavalry from Fort Yates, under Captain E.G. Fechet, followed to about ten miles from

Sitting Bull's camp, where they waited to support the police.

At dawn, the policemen emerged from trees fringing the river and rushed Sitting Bull's log cabin, waking him up and telling him that they had come to take him to the agency. The chief offered no resistance, but got dressed and, surrounded by the policemen, left the house. Outside, a huge crowd of his Hunkpapa followers, whose cabins and tipis were clustered around his home, gathered excitedly about the chief, trying to protect him and urging him not to go with the agency police. Heeding their cries, Sitting Bull suddenly halted and refused to go further. As the police, headed by Lieutenant Bull Head, tried to pull and push him along, the crowd became wild with anger. A shot rang out, striking Bull Head in the side. As he fell, he fired his revolver, hitting Sitting Bull in the chest. Another policeman, Sergeant Red Tomahawk, who had been pushing Sitting Bull from behind, shot the chief in the back of the head. Sitting Bull, the great chief and medicine man of the Hunkpapa Sioux and to the whites the most famous and feared Indian in the country, dropped to the ground, dead.

Consternation struck the Indians who had been swirling about him. In the altercation that followed, the chief's enraged people attacked the policemen with guns, clubs, and knives. The police fought back, and men on both sides were killed and wounded. During the struggle, the noise of the gunshots and the shouting and crying were like signals to Sitting Bull's trained horse, which Buffalo Bill had given him during his days with the Wild West show, and incongruously it began to perform circus tricks. At length, Sitting Bull's followers, mourning the death of their chief, withdrew into the trees along the river, and the battered policemen retreated with their casualties into Sitting Bull's cabin and sent a messenger to Fechet's troops for help.

The soldiers hurried to the scene, engaging in a brief skirmish with scores of angry Hunkpapas who resisted them from the trees lining the river and from a knob near the settlement. Firing their Hotchkiss gun at the Indians' positions, Fechet's men finally forced the Sioux to withdraw up the Grand River, then returned to the Standing Rock agency with the dead and wounded policemen and the body of Sitting Bull—which was wrapped in canvas and buried unceremoniously in the post cemetery at Fort Yates.

Afraid that Sitting Bull's followers who had retreated from Fechet's troops would pose a new peril by joining, and thus strengthening, the Ghost Dancers on the Cheyenne River reservation or at the Stronghold on the Pine Ridge reservation, McLaughlin sent messengers to find the fugitives and persuade them to come in to the Standing Rock agency. The emissaries overtook the destitute and wounded refugees, leaderless, hungry, and frightened, on the Cheyenne River reservation and managed to talk about half of them into returning to Standing Rock. The rest, numbering close to 200, continued their flight south, hoping to find safety with Big Foot's band of Miniconjou Ghost Dancers on the Cheyenne River along the southern boundary of the reservation.

Among the whites, Big Foot was considered almost as dangerous a threat to peace as Sitting Bull had been. The leader of a group of devout Ghost Dancers, whom white observers had regarded as "wild" and defiant, Big Foot had moved his band far up the Cheyenne River to get away from the agency and to practice the new religion without interference. In the following weeks, a military emissary had been able to

19. *Sitting Bull, c. 1883.*
20. *Indian Policemen, c. 1890 (?). The man in the center is Red Tomahawk.*
21. *Sitting Bull's Cane, Sioux, c. 1885.*

induce the only other important body of Ghost Dancers on the reservation, led by Big Foot's friend, Hump, to give up their dancing and go in to the agency. Hump's defection had disheartened Big Foot, and he, too, along with a number of his followers, had stopped dancing and turned away from the Messiah's religion. Whites were unaware of his change of heart, however, and because his band, still composed of many ardent Ghost Dancers, lived in freedom and continued to avoid control by the agent, they viewed him as a menace.

Nevertheless, Lieutenant Colonel Edwin V. Sumner, the commander of some 200 troops stationed just west of Big Foot's band to protect white-owned ranches on the Cheyenne and Belle Fourche rivers outside the reservation's boundaries, visited with Big Foot on several occasions and found the chief and his people peaceful and offering no problems. If anything, the officer decided, Big Foot was a cooperative Indian, able to exercise a helpful, moderating influence on those elements in the band who were still dancing under the leadership of a zealous medicine man named Yellow Bird.

22. *Jacket, man's, Sioux, c. 1890.*

During the second week of December, Big Foot, whom the various Sioux tribes knew for his ability as a peacemaker in settling disputes among themselves, received a message from Red Cloud and other Oglala chiefs, offering him 100 ponies if he would come to Pine Ridge and help restore harmony among different factions on that reservation. The day, however, when the government issued rations and annuities at the Cheyenne River agency was approaching, and Big Foot and his fellow council members decided that they would first lead their people, who were running out of food, down to the agency to draw their much-needed rations and would then determine whether to accept the Oglala chiefs' invitation.

On December 15, Big Foot's band started downriver to the Cheyenne River agency. It was the day that Sitting Bull was killed. Two days later, Sumner received a vaguely-worded message from department headquarters, informing him that the arrest of Big Foot would be "desirable," but conveying no order to him to make the arrest. Shortly afterward, the officer learned the reason for his superiors' suddenly-heightened interest in Big Foot. Scouts informed him that a large body of Hunkpapa refugees, fleeing from Standing Rock after Sitting Bull's death, were about to link up with Big Foot's band and intended to ask the Miniconjous to go with them to the Oglala and Brule Ghost Dancers at the Stronghold on Pine Ridge. At that moment, General Brooke at Pine Ridge was about to send a force of some 500 "friendly" Sioux to the Stronghold to try to persuade Kicking Bear, Short Bull, and the rest of the dancers who were still there to come in to the agency. The last thing he would welcome would be the reinforcing of the Pine Ridge Ghost Dancers by Big Foot's Miniconjous and the Standing Rock Hunkpapas.

Sumner vacillated, not certain what he should do, then started his troops down the Cheyenne River after Big Foot. On December 21, he overtook the Miniconjou band, finding that it had already met the fleeing Hunkpapas. Their report of the murder of Sitting Bull and of the fighting with the Army at Standing Rock had alarmed the Miniconjous, thoroughly frightening the women and children and making the men angry. The tension had mounted higher when Big Foot had learned at almost the same time that a force of soldiers, other than Sumner's, was marching toward the Miniconjous, up the Cheyenne River from the direction of the agency. They were four companies of the 7th Infantry under Colonel H.C. Merriam, ordered to effect a junction with Sumner. The Indians had become confused. Why was the Army threatening and killing the Sioux, who were doing nothing but dancing peacefully? The upshot had been that most of the refugee Hunkpapas had decided to avoid further trouble and go to the Cheyenne River agency. Only 38 of Sitting Bull's people, Sumner discovered, had joined Big Foot's band.

Planning to keep Big Foot under observation, Sumner had no difficulty persuading the chief to turn his people around and, escorted by his troops, return upriver. Even though they risked hunger and starvation by not drawing their rations, the Miniconjous were too uneasy about the intentions of the soldiers coming upriver to want to continue toward the agency. On the way back with Sumner, their apprehension intensified, and when they reached the site of their own village, they were so fearful and wrought up that to avoid a fight, Sumner left them there overnight, with a promise from Big Foot, whom Sumner trusted, that he would restrain the young men and come to Sumner's army camp the next day for a council.

That night, Sumner received a message from General Miles, who had established his headquarters at Rapid City. Miles warned him to watch out for some hostile Indians who were reported to be coming down from the north to threaten the whites' settlements. Believing that Sumner had already arrested Big Foot and his band—although Sumner had never received orders to do so—Miles also told him to bring the prisoners to Fort Meade near Rapid City.

Sumner faced a predicament. In the Miniconjous' high state of tension, any attempt to force them to go to Fort Meade as prisoners, he felt, would result in a bloody battle with a large loss of Indians' lives and the probable escape of many of the most dangerous warriors. Moreover, he did not think that he had enough men to move the unwilling band to Fort Meade and at the same time cope with hostile Indians who were supposed to be coming down from the north (that report, eventually, proved to be false). The best solution, Sumner decided, was to induce Big Foot—about whose situation and motives he was more realistic than Miles—to take his people in to the Cheyenne River agency where he had originally been heading.

The next morning, the Standing Rock Indians, fearing that they had got themselves into a trap between the troops of Sumner and Merriam, fled from Big Foot's village, and the Miniconjou chief postponed visiting Sumner while he tried unsuccessfully to find the frightened Hunkpapas. When Big Foot failed to appear at Sumner's camp as he had promised to do, the officer sent an interpreter and a local white rancher, who knew Big Foot, to find out what the trouble was. Far from diplomatic, the rancher panicked the Indians by telling them that they were about to be sent to Fort Bennett, the army post near the Cheyenne River agency, and that if they refused to go, the soldiers would shoot them.

Ignoring the appointment with Sumner, the alarmed members of the band's council met with Big Foot to consider their options, deciding finally to head south immediately to the protection of the chiefs at Pine Ridge. At first, Big Foot, who was not feeling well, resisted making the long journey, preferring to go peaceably to the Cheyenne River agency. But the other headmen argued for accepting the Oglalas' invitation, and Big Foot finally agreed. During the night of December 23, the band struck off for the south, leaving in their rear Sumner's troops, as well as those of Merriam.

Big Foot's escape from the forces on the Cheyenne River infuriated General Miles, who was now sure not only that the Miniconjou chief was one of the most cunning and treacherous of all the Ghost Dance leaders, but that he was taking his people to the Stronghold to stiffen the resistance of the Brules and Oglalas, just when General Brooke was beginning to have success in talking the last of those holdouts into giving themselves up. Determined to intercept and seize Big Foot before he could reach the Stronghold, the Army organized a huge search for him. Covered by a swarm of reporters, who had flocked into the bleak, muddy agency town of Pine Ridge to be present at the surrender of the followers of Kicking Bear and Short Bull, the campaign to capture Big Foot became of almost equal news interest, acquiring the drama of a hunt for an elusive band of religiously-crazed Sioux and their dangerously fanatic chief.

Making their way south out on the Plains, desperately trying to avoid being overtaken or cut off by troops, the lonely band of some 350 Miniconjous were anything but belligerent or dangerous. The Indians' journey across the hard winter ground and through the silent, eroded Badlands to the White River on the northern border of the Pine Ridge reservation was one of suffering and hardship. Buffeted by icy winds and snow squalls, the people froze and were hungry and sick. Big Foot's illness became worse, and his family wrapped him in blankets and laid him in the box of a bouncing, jolting wagon. On December 24, he developed pneumonia.

Most of all, the people feared the soldiers, who were all about them, but whom they managed to evade. Time and again, they slipped past searching bodies of troops, first of Colonel Eugene A. Carr's veteran 6th Cavalry, which had been called to South Dakota from Arizona and New Mexico to help suppress the Sioux, and then of black troopers of the 9th Cavalry, dispatched from Pine Ridge under Major Guy V. Henry. At last, the Indians entered the northern part of the Pine Ridge reservation and sent three riders to the Oglala chiefs near the Pine Ridge agency, announcing that they would soon reach their camps and telling them that Big Foot was very ill. In response, Indian messengers returned with word that Kicking Bear and Short Bull had at last led the Ghost Dancers out of the Stronghold in the Badlands, that they were all on their way to the Pine Ridge agency, and that Kicking Bear would like the Miniconjous to time their arrival at the agency to coincide with his own.

At his Pine Ridge headquarters, meanwhile, General Brooke, pleased that the Ghost Dancers at the Stronghold had finally given up and were on their way to the agency, had learned that Big Foot's band had reached the Pine Ridge reservation and was heading not for the Stronghold, but southwestward toward Porcupine and Wounded Knee creeks and the Pine Ridge agency. He immediately directed Major Samuel Whitside, with four troops of the 7th Cavalry and two Hotchkiss guns, to intercept and capture the band, take away the Indians' horses and guns, and hold the prisoners for further orders.

Riding east to the valley of Wounded Knee Creek, Whitside and his men established a camp near a trading post and sent out some Oglala Indian scouts toward the northeast to locate Big Foot's band. Late in the morning of December 28, contact was made, when four of the scouts were surprised at Porcupine Creek by an advance groups of the Miniconjous. When the main party of Indians came up, Big Foot sent two of Whitside's scouts back to the officer to inform him that his people were peaceful and would move directly to the soldiers' encampment on Wounded Knee Creek. Mistrusting the Indians—who had slipped out of Sumner's hands and evaded other troops—Whitside ignored the message and, ordering his men to saddle up, hurried them across the hills toward Porcupine Creek. A little after 2 p.m., they intercepted the Miniconjous, and after a discussion with the sick chief—as related earlier — escorted the Indians back toward Wounded Knee Creek.

Racing ahead of the column, a courier carried the news of the capture of Big Foot to Wounded Knee. From there, word was relayed by a series of flashing heliograph mirrors to General Brooke at his Pine Ridge headquarters, 17 miles away by

23. *General Brooke's Camp, Pine Ridge Agency, c. 1891.*

the reservation's roads. In the same message, Brooke was asked to dispatch more troops to help Whitside overawe the Indians and persuade them to give up their arms peacefully. Brooke immediately turned out Colonel James W. Forsyth, commander of the 7th Cavalry, with four more troops of that regiment, two more Hotchkiss guns, an interpreter, and another body of Oglala scouts, and sent them off to reinforce Whitside. Once the Indians were disarmed, Brooke told Forsyth, he was to order Whitside to march them to the railroad at Gordon, Nebraska, from where they would be sent to Omaha for imprisonment or exile.

Accompanying Forsyth to witness the disarming of the Miniconjous was a small group of civilians, including a Catholic missionary, a Pine Ridge trader, and three newspapermen. Most of the correspondents at Pine Ridge, including the reporter-artist, Frederic Remington, who was on assignment for *Harper's Weekly*, remained at the agency, deciding that the expected arrival and surrender of Kicking Bear and the holdouts from the Stronghold would be bigger news than the seizure of Big Foot.

At Wounded Knee, Whitside's camp had been pitched in the valley between the creek on the east and a hill on the west. Coming from the northeast, the Indians were led south past the rows of cavalry tents to an open flat beneath the hill, where they erected their own village in an arc of tipis. A shallow, dry ravine with steep walls ran from west to east along the rear of their village, opening into Wounded Knee Creek.

At the south edge of the cavalry camp, which was separated from the Indians' village by about 100 yards of open land, Whitside had a large wall tent, heated by a camp stove, set up for Big Foot. At the same time, the officer ringed the Indians' village tightly with sentinels from two of his troops and placed his Hotchkiss guns on the hill to command the tipi village. About 8:30 that night, Forsyth arrived with his reinforcements. The colonel had his men bivouac north of Whitside's camp and added his Hotchkiss guns to the two already on the hill above the Indians. To deal with 350 Sioux, Forsyth, who took over command from Whitside, possessed a force of slightly more than 500 soldiers and Oglala Scouts.

During the evening, Forsyth and his officers of the 7th Cavalry, some of whom had fought the Sioux at the Little Bighorn 15 years before, opened a small keg of whiskey which the trader had brought from Pine Ridge and drank to the capitulation of Big Foot. Later, their celebration led to an accusation—contested, and probably untrue—that the officers were drunk during the events of the next morning. (The enlisted men, too, were accused of being drunk, but none of them had participated in the drinking). Of more substance, perhaps, was a charge that the officers and many of the men of the 7th looked on their disarming of Big Foot's people the next day as a measure of revenge for what the Sioux had done to Custer and their regiment at the Little Bighorn. Whether it was a motivation for the savagery of what occurred, however, will never be known.

At any rate, if the troops were celebratory, expecting an easy and victorious time the next morning, the Indians were just the opposite. The patrolling sentinels surrounding their village, the guns pointing down at them from the hill, and the arrival of Forsyth's additional troops all seemed to be ominous signs. Many of the people stayed awake much of the night, filled with apprehension and fear.

At daybreak, Forsyth distributed rations of bacon and hardtack to the Miniconjous and, soon afterward, had his interpreter summon all the Indian men to a council in the large square in front of Big Foot's tent. Nervous and uneasy, the Sioux were herded into a close-packed, semicircular line, facing the cavalry camp, with their backs to the worried Indian women and children whom they had left in the village. To impress the Indians that resistance would result in their annihilation, Forsyth had deployed his troops in commanding positions on all sides of the council grounds.

Tension, already high, mounted when Forsyth informed the Indians that he wanted them to surrender their guns. Remembering Sitting Bull's murder, and fearing that, without guns, they could be slaughtered, the Miniconjous hesitated. Two of them went into Big Foot's tent to seek his advice and were apparently told by him to give up their old guns and keep their good ones. Returning, they told the other Indians what their chief had said. A short time later, when Forsyth sent a first group of Indians back to their tipis with orders to return with their rifles, they brought back two broken carbines, claiming that those were the only guns they had.

The day before, Whitside and his men had seen many of the Indians carrying good Winchesters. Realizing that the Sioux were deceiving him, and beginning to fear trouble from them, Forsyth had Big Foot carried out of his tent and placed on the ground in front of the Indians. At the same time, he moved Troops K and B of the 7th Regiment close up behind the Miniconjous. Forming an L-shaped line on the south and west sides of the council square, the bluecoats cut the Indians off

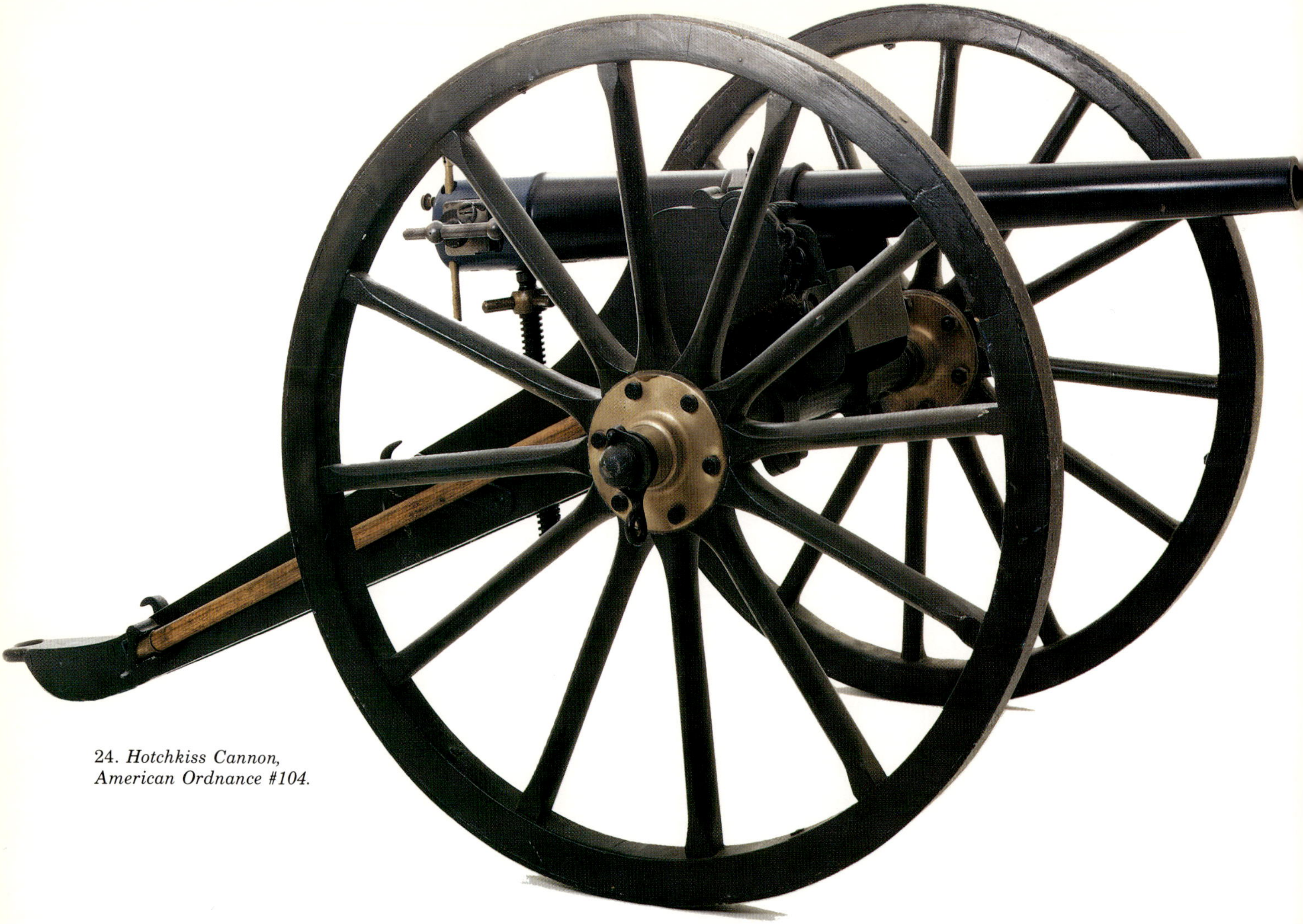

24. *Hotchkiss Cannon,*
American Ordnance #104.

from the tipi village. When Big Foot insisted in a weak and barely audible voice that his people had given up all the guns they possessed, Forsyth told him he did not believe him and detailed some of his men to search the Indian village.

As the troopers went through the tipis, seizing guns, crowbars, awls, and anything that could be used as a weapon, the Indians became increasingly restless and angry. Some of them—worried about the women and children in the village—tried to get through the line of dismounted cavalrymen, but were held back. A few wore the Ghost Shirts of their religion, and their old medicine man, Yellow Bird, who had been making the troopers nervous by singing and dancing through the crowd, occasionally scooping up a handful of dust and throwing it at the soldiers, began crying to the Miniconjous, assuring them that the white men's bullets would not be able to harm them.

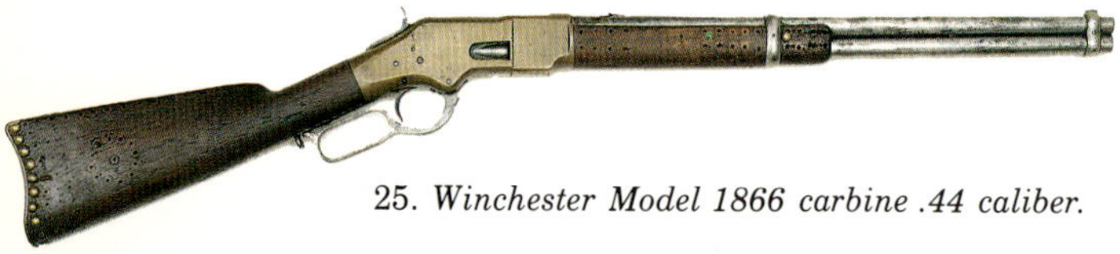

25. *Winchester Model 1866 carbine .44 caliber.*

When the troopers finished going through the village, having turned up 38 rifles, Forsyth told the Indians that he wanted them to open their blankets and satisfy him that they had no concealed weapons. The older men came forward at once, pulled off their blankets, and showed that they carried no weapons. The younger men, however, began to grow excited. Three of them were searched, and a Winchester and another rifle, hidden beneath their blankets, were taken from them. With his voice rising higher and higher, Yellow Bird began to whirl about furiously in his dance. The commotion alarmed the troopers, many of whom were recent recruits, filled with fear of Indians. At the rear of the Miniconjous' circle a deaf Indian raised a rifle above his head with both hands and shouted that he had paid money for it and would not give it up without being paid for it. Two soldiers grabbed him from behind and tried to wrestle the gun away from him. Just as the medicine man scooped up some more dust and threw it in the air as if it were a signal, the deaf man's rifle, pointing harmlessly toward the sky, went off.

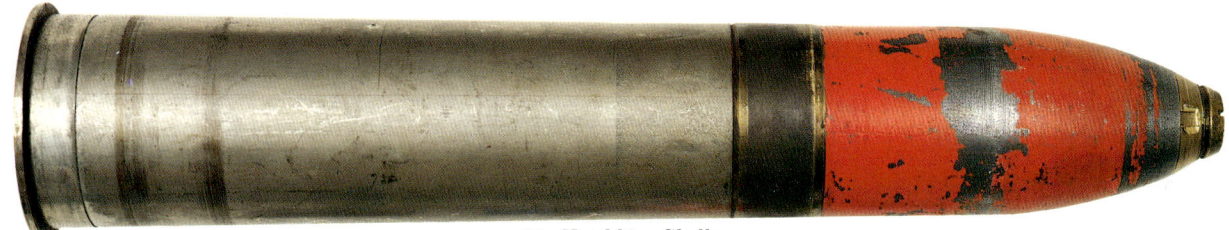

26. *Hotchkiss Shell*

In an instant, the fears of both sides exploded in uncontrollable violence. Each survivor of that morning had his or her own flashes of memory of what happened next. Some said that five or six young Indians threw aside their blankets and fired point-blank at the bluecoats of Troop K, who were standing between the Indians and the tipi village. Others said that the nervous members of both Troop K and Troop B, reacting instinctively to the shot from the deaf Indian's rifle, sent a volley crashing into the Miniconjous. Once started, the fury could not be stopped.

The council site became a scene of horror, as the Indians and troopers fought at close range, shooting at each other as fast as they could. Bullets flew in every direction, cutting down Indians and soldiers in heaps. In their frenzied fire, the troopers in the L-shaped line hit fellow-troopers, and Indians, missing the soldiers, sent bullets ripping into the tipi village, where women with their babies and older children were screaming and running about, trying to get away.

When the Indians ran out of bullets, they rushed at the soldiers, fighting hand-to-hand with knives and bare hands and breaking through the troopers' line. Many raced to the tipi village, but others ran to the northeast or to the west. During the pandemonium in the council square, the troops whom Forsyth had deployed around the area, as well as the gunners on the hill, watched in frozen shock, unable to fire into the swirling mass for fear of killing their own men. (Later, Forsyth would be court-martialled for the inept deployment of his men, many of whom were killed or wounded by their own crossfire on the council square). Once the Indians broke loose from the soldiers and raced away from the square, the Hotchkiss guns and the outlying troops, mostly mounted, went into action. From their perch on the hill, the gunners sent explosive shells into the Indian village and against groups of fleeing Miniconjous, ripping apart men, women, and children with pieces of flying shrapnel. Those who kept going, uninjured, were pursued and cut down by the fresh troops, maddened by what they viewed as the Indians' treachery.

On the council ground, Big Foot and most of the elder Miniconjou headmen were among the first casualties. The chief was shot in the head and killed instantly as he tried to rise from where he had been lying on his back. Yellow Bird, the medicine man, disappeared in a tent from which he sniped at the troopers until they riddled the tent with bullets and then set it on fire, roasting the religious leader to death.

Running from the tipi village while the fighting raged on the council square, some of the women and children got into wagons and headed up a road that led toward the northwest. Seeing that there were no men with them, the troops at first let them get away, then went after them, trapping, killing, and capturing small groups of them a mile and more from Wounded Knee. The bulk of those in the village made their way toward the rear of the tipis, then, followed by the Indian men who had broken through the line of troops on the council grounds, ran south, crossing the ravine to open ground, where three lines of Forsyth's troops and Indian scouts opened fire on them. With shells from the Hotchkiss guns exploding among them and the soldier's rifles flaming at them from the front, the Indians were literally mowed down in clumps of dead and wounded. The survivors retreated into the ravine and, pursued by the soldiers, ran along it in both directions.

In the smoke, dust, exploding shells, and flying pieces of metal, a few Indians tried to resist. Here and there in the ravine, groups of Miniconjous

27. *Intrenching/Hunting Knife, U.S. Army, c. 1880.*

28. *Gathering Up the Dead at the Battlefield at Wounded Knee, S.D., 1891.*

29. *Chief Big Foot's Knife, c. 1880.*

fought back briefly, defending women and their babies and children, who tried to claw shelters for themselves in the dirt walls. Assisted by the Hotchkiss guns, the troopers attacked them furiously, wiping them out or forcing them to surrender. As the resistance in the valley died out and the carnage ended, Forsyth sent soldiers hurrying westward to search for Indians who had escaped. In the upper part of the ravine and elsewhere, desperate refugees were found and killed in episodes of unrestrained viciousness. One group of troopers ran into a party of 150 mounted Oglala and Brule warriors who, having heard the sound of fighting, had ridden from the agency to help the Miniconjous. After a brief exchange of fire, the Oglalas and Brules realized that they were too late and withdrew.

By noon, the struggle was over. Big Foot's band had been all but annihilated. Leaving the Indians dead where they lay—bunched on the council square and scattered in knots up and down the ravine and across the open ground—Forsyth gathered his own dead and, putting the wounded of both sides into wagons, marched back to the Pine Ridge agency, where General Brooke and others hailed the fight as a stirring victory.

That night, a heavy snow began to fall, and in the silent valley of Wounded Knee Creek, a white blanket covered the Indian dead. Three days later, a detail went to the field and buried the frozen bodies of 84 men and boys, 44 women, and 18 children in a large grave on the hill where the four Hotchkiss guns and been.

The reporters who had accompanied Forsyth sent the story of what had happened to the outside world. Some editors congratulated the Army on a glorious triumph over dangerously hostile Indians. But others, criticizing the attack on surrounded and surrendered Indians, and the killing of Indian women, babies, and children, accused the 7th Cavalry of having sought revenge on the Sioux for the defeat at the Little Bighorn by perpetrating a massacre at Wounded Knee.

To Indians, the issue of whether it was an accidental fight or a massacre has never been in question, but the United States government, allowing the Army to define the action, continues to this day to insist officially that Wounded Knee was not a massacre, but a battle that resulted from misunderstanding on both sides. Although it is difficult to imagine what misunderstandings possessed the Indians about the whites, it is certain that the white ignorance about the Indians, together with a 400-year heritage of avarice, racism, and conflict, were at the root of Wounded Knee. The more immediate causes ranged from the unwarranted hysteria of the agents and the white population to the sending of troops onto the reservations and the mistakes of Miles and some of his officers. What resulted—especially the brutal hunting down and slaughter after the initial desperate fighting on the council grounds—fits the dictionary definition of a massacre: "savage and indiscriminate killing."

There were other ramifications. For several days after Wounded Knee, angry Oglala and Brule warriors made scattered attacks on various buildings at the agency and on other centers on the reservation, causing a number of casualties to the troops. At the same time, Kicking Bear, Short Bull, and the other Ghost Dancers who had been coming in from the Stronghold took fright at Big Foot's fate and, accompanied by several thousand Indians who fled from the agency, returned to the Badlands. Miles kept them under pressure, however, and on January 15, 1891, Kicking Bear and the other remaining Ghost Dance leaders finally surrendered. Their fate was a surprise to them. Instead of being sent to prison, they were hired by Buffalo Bill and, with the approval of the Secretary of War, toured Europe for a year, earning money as star attractions of the Wild West show.

The promises of Wovoka's religion and of the Ghost Dance could not long survive what had happened at Wounded Knee. The Ghost Shirts had not repelled the soldiers' bullets, and the Indians gradually turned away from the prayers, dances, sacred songs, and visions of a world without whites. But more than the Messiah's religion was trampled on and gunned away in the tragedy at Wounded Knee. With the death of Big Foot's Miniconjous, there expired the last free band of Sioux Indians. From then on, the Sioux would know for a certainty that they could no longer hope to be masters of their lives, able to exist and worship as a free people.

As the Oglala holy man, Black Elk, later said, the nation's hoop was broken and scattered at Wounded Knee. There was no center any longer, and the sacred tree was dead. As for the soldiers who shattered the hoop at Wounded Knee, 18 of them received Congressional Medals of Honor for what they had done.

30. *Sioux Indian War Medal, Nebraska State National Guard, 1890-1891 (left), Congressional Medal of Honor, undesignated, c. 1890 (middle), Indian War Medal with matching chest ribbon (right).*

31. *Kicking Bear, Young Man Afraid, Standing Bear, Pine Ridge Agency, January 1891.*

32. *Sioux Family, c. 1890.*

CRISIS AND CREATIVITY: THE GHOST DANCE ART STYLE

by
Trudy Thomas

The great underlying principle of the Ghost Dance doctrine is that . . . the whole Indian race, living and dead, will be reunited upon a regenerated earth, to live a life of aboriginal happiness, forever free from death, disease, and misery.[1]

Before 1880, the Great Plains of North America were home to mounted Native American warriors who fought for defense and personal achievement, and displayed the symbols of their self-determination on their weapons, on the "walls" of their homes, and on their clothing. In the old days, native Plains people followed buffalo herds on horseback, hunting the animals for meat and fashioning clothing, shelter and tools from the horns, bones and hides. Successful hunters traded their surplus to other Native American people and to European Americans for such items as corn, shells, pottery, beads, bells, cloth, dyes, metal buckles and jewelry, axes, knives, guns and ammunition. The Indian Wars of 1850 to 1870, which set Native American people against an ever-rising tide of European immigrants, brought to a close the florescence of this traditional native Plains cultural pattern.

By the end of the 19th century, life had changed markedly for Indian people living on the North American Plains. The Plains warriors had been beaten in battles they could not win—overcome by starvation, new diseases, and seemingly endless waves of European immigrants protected by the United States Army. The buffalo were nearly gone, virtually exterminated by white hunters, and by 1880 most native people had been forcibly settled onto reservations and were no longer allowed to follow their traditional way of life. Death rates were extremely high. It was into this setting that hope of a new world order was offered. At some time immediately preceding the year 1890, the Ghost Dance religion was introduced to Plains people by a Paiute prophet from Nevada named Wovoka.

As native cultures strained under the onslaught, the Ghost Dance religion of 1890 spread throughout the Plains. Ghost Dancers envisioned a renewed world characterized by resurrection of the Indian dead, increase of the buffalo, and a return to their old way of life. The most clearly evident visual symbols of their fervent hopes were garments fashioned of hide or cloth, and painted with a variety of motifs including the crescent moon, stars, multi-colored lines, rainbows, dragonflies, turtles, and birds with wings outstretched and lightning bolts coming from their bodies. Ghost Dance garments were decorated with images which their owners had received in visions, and were worn by men, women and children alike, who believed that the so-called "bullet-proof shirts" possessed the power to protect them from harm.

The Ghost Dance of 1890 was but one of many revitalization movements which followed in the

33. *Dress, muslin, Sioux, c. 1885.*

34. Dress, deerskin, Arapaho/Southern Plains, c. 1890.

wake of European expansion in North America and, indeed, throughout the world. Some of the better known of these are the Melanesian Cargo Cult, the Smohalla Cult of the Columbia Plateau, the Handsome Lake religion of the Seneca, the California Bole Maru, and the Pueblo Revolt of 1680. The 1890 Plains Ghost Dance was itself preceded by an earlier, less well-known, Ghost Dance movement in 1870.

Like other movements before it, the Ghost Dance of 1890 was a response by indigenous people to the disruptive methods and devastating effects of European expansionism. Thus, the movement can be interpreted as an attempt by Plains people to re-orient to changing conditions. Similarly, the art style which the Ghost Dance inspired can be understood as a symbolic expression of attempts by Plains Indian people to come to terms with a new age.

The Old and the New: Ghost Dance Art as a Restyled Synthesis

It might be said that the Ghost Dance art style was a synthesis of old and new ideas extant on the North American Plains during the last half of the 19th century. The technical and aesthetic achievements of Ghost Dance clothing reflect some of the cross-cultural exchanges that were regularly occurring between Indian societies and European-American culture during this time period. For instance, the use of rows and scatters of white stars on a dark ground can perhaps be explained in terms of the adoption by the native artisans of the American flag.[2] On some garments, imported items such as glass beads and metal bells were simply added to traditionally constructed hide garments as subsidiary decorative elements. Other Ghost Dance outfits were fashioned almost entirely of imported goods, by choice, or to supplement dwindling supplies of traditional raw materials. Overall, Native American Ghost Dance clothing was a creative amalgamation of old and new features.

Ghost Dance garments were often fashioned from the same materials as were traditional items of wearing apparel; that is, from a variety of items, some of which were indigenous to the Plains and others that were imported from elsewhere. Imported items included European-made cloth and thread, metal bells, Venetian glass beads, and cowrie shells from the Indian Ocean. Material used for the manufacture of Ghost Dance garments and other kinds of wearing apparel was sometimes native tanned leather and, in other instances, imported cotton cloth. While chemical assessments of the paints used to decorate Ghost Dance garments have yet to be made, it is likely that at least some of the coloring agents will be identified as imported commercial products.

The cut of most Ghost Dance style garments was like that of traditional Plains wearing apparel made of leather. Most cloth and leather Ghost shirts as well as women's cloth Ghost Dance dresses were patterned after men's leather shirts from the Southern Plains. Points of similarity include closed sleeves and side seams, set-in sleeves, use of fringes, and emphasis upon painting as the primary decorative medium. Side gussets, however, were usually added to cloth Ghost Dance dresses to provide extra skirt width.

Perhaps the most striking parellel between Ghost Dance and traditional clothing styles is a large triangular area which extends from a point at the center of the chest or torso to the tops of the shoulders. On men's shirts from the Southern Plains this form is a large triangular neck flap, often bounded by long fringes. On Ghost Dance garments the triangular area is often not a flap at all, but instead, is a shape delineated by two painted or fringed lines drawn from a point at the center of the chest or torso to the tops of the shoulders. One or more motifs were typically painted within this triangular area on Ghost Dance garments; though in some instances, motifs radiate over nearly the entire surface of the garment in a "bird's-eye view" arrangement reminiscent of traditional Plains figurative hide painting.

Women's leather Ghost Dance dresses were exceptions to this format. Ghost Dance dresses made of tanned animal hides were fashioned in the manner of traditional three skin Plains dresses, with the hide forming the bodice attached laterally to longitudinal skirt sections. No triangular area was delineated on the upper body of these traditionally constructed leather dresses. Layout of painted motifs was, however, the same as other Ghost Dance garments; that is, a centrally located motif was generally flanked by two symmetrically placed but not necessarily identical motifs.

Ghost Dance art emphasized different subject matter than did the biographical and historical accounts painted onto buffalo robes and ledger book pages, but the manner of portraying figurative subjects on two-dimensional surfaces is similar. Perspective is typically lacking in the 1890 Ghost Dance painting style, as it is in much of traditional Plains painting; backgrounds and details of environmental settings are only minimally indicated, if they are shown at all. The use of ground lines and landscapes are European-inspired innovations which were not incorporated into Ghost Dance art. Human or animal figures on Ghost Dance garments are drawn in realistic detail with anatomically correct proportions in the manner typical of post-1860 Plains painting.[3] Colors on Ghost Dance garments are flat, as in older examples of Plains painting, with little or no shading or modeling; outlining is common. Modeling and shading are European-American conventions which were not adapted to the Ghost Dance art style. Because Ghost Dance art was inspired by personal visionary experience, colors are not always lifelike, but instead, are based upon symbolic meaning, upon personal interpretation of the vision which was the source for the painted design, or on color availability.

Trade with Europeans and with other Native American tribes had long been important to Plains people for the purpose of providing market outlets for Plains goods (such as buffalo hides), and as a means for acquiring items not readily available at home. Thus, although the stimulus for the development of the Ghost Dance art style lay in dire events of the late 19th century, the creative amalgamation of old and new elements which comprised the Ghost Dance tradition was not unique. Rather, the practice of combining the

35. *Dress, deerskin, Arapaho, c. 1890.*

familiar and the unfamiliar, the old and the new, was part of a pre-existing way of life.

Ghost Dance Designs

Four motifs were consistently used to decorate the majority of Ghost Dance garments: crescent, star (including Maltese cross as Morning Star), bird, and multi-colored rainbow lines call "trails" (drawn around the torso, arms and legs, and across the chest). Some shirts and dresses were painted with only these designs, while others were decorated with a number of other motifs used in combination with one or more of these four. Other designs include dots, discs, rings, concentric circles, rayed circles, "bull's eyes" (i.e., dots within rings), horses, human figures, bows and arrows, carnivorous animals, hunted hoofed animals, plants or trees, pipes, turtles, rabbits, spider webs, dragon flies, forked zigzags, and rainbows. Carnivorous animals, hunted animals, horses, and weapons of war are rare on Ghost Dance garments.

The crescent moon or the Morning Star (represented as a Maltese cross) were usually painted onto the center of the chest and back of

Ghost Dance outfits, while birds and stars frequently appear in flanking positions. Rainbow "trails" were painted around cuffs, midriffs, hemlines, elbows or upper arms, and shoulder-arm junctures of Ghost Dance garments. Trails were also often painted diagonally from a point (or a motif) at center chest and/or the center of the back to the tops of the shoulders and down the arms. Colored lines (often with fringes attached) might also be drawn down the sides of the garment.

37. *Shirt, muslin, Gros Ventre, 50/4320, c. 1890.*

36. *Shirt, muslin, Sioux, c. 1890.*

diamonds, dots, and four and five-pointed configurations. The older method of depicting stars was with four points.[8] The Morning Star was depicted as a four-pointed star by the Sioux people,[9] and the Cheyenne symbolized the Morning Star both as a Maltese cross and as a diamond (a square turned angle up).[10] Stars on Ghost Dance garments were drawn with four, five, or more points, and as Maltese crosses.

Crescent

On the Plains, the moon was generally represented by a crescent. As we have seen, the crescent moon was a favorite design on Ghost Dance garments, and was also painted onto the bodies of principal performers in a number of Arapaho and Cheyenne Sun Dance ceremonies observed between 1901 and 1969. Association of the crescent moon with the Sun Dance is seen in other contexts among the Assiniboine, who carved a crescent moon into the center pole of their Sun Dance lodge,[4] and the Alberta Cree, who painted a crescent onto their Sun Dance lodge center pole above the image of a blue Thunderbird.[5]

Star

In some Plains contexts, stars were used as symbols of concepts relating to the creation and perpetuation of life on earth. The Ponca used a set of tatoos featuring a four-point star, a crescent moon, the sun, and crosses to symbolize an appeal for perpetuation of all life, and human life in particular.[5] Pawnee people depicted the home of the Supreme Being, Tirawahat, by means of a four-point star; it was at Tirawahat's discretion that Morning Star initiated the actions which culminated in the creation of the Pawnee earth and sun.[7]

On the Plains, stars were depicted in a number of ways including crosses, Maltese crosses,

38. *Leggings, men's, Arapaho, c. 1890.*

Trails

On Ghost Dance garments trails are identified as colored lines which encircle or delineate waist/midriff, hemline or ankle cuff, wrist/cuff, elbow/mid-arm/upper arm, and shoulder/arm junctures. Trails drawn onto the bodies of

39. Star Hair Ornament, Arapaho, c. 1890 (?).

principal Cheyenne Sun Dance participants are defined as the paths or roads which lead to the homes of the four Sacred Persons of the Four Directions of the World who are the Guardians of Creation.[11]

Bird

The majority of the birds depicted on Ghost Dance garments can be identified as crows or ravens, magpies, and eagles or hawks.

In his spiritual manifestation, the eagle was believed to take the form of Thunderbird, and was considered to be a bearer of messages between the spirit world and man.[12] Some people regarded the eagle to be the most powerful of all the birds with the ability to protect and cure humans.[13]

For the Pawnee, the hawk was a symbol of bravery and was regarded as the messenger of Morning Star, who created the sun and came to command lightning, thunder, wind and clouds.[14] It was from Morning Star that all Pawnee warriors were deemed to derive their powers to succeed.[15] The Cheyenne regarded hawks as well as eagles as having the power to protect a person from injury.[16]

Ravens were regarded by the Santee Sioux to be messengers of the Four Winds which are themselves the messengers of the supernatural powers residing at the four quarters of the world.[17] The Cheyenne regarded ravens to be capable of assisting in locating buffalo.[18]

The crow and magpie were reported to have special significance for the Ghost Dance.[19] Magpies were revered by Ghost Dancers because they are native to Nevada, the home of Wovoka, the Ghost Dance prophet, and the crow is said to have been revered as the sacred bird of the Ghost Dance because its black color was regarded as symbolic of death.[20] Crows were believed to function as messengers from the spirit world for Ghost Dancers.[21]

Crow feathers were worn on the heads of Ghost Dancers in the belief that the feathers would act as wings to enable dancers to escape the dying world below by flying to the new earth above.[22] Furthermore, according to Ghost Dance belief, a crow acted as the leader of spirit armies who marched to rejoin departed friends in the spirit land above, and in Ghost Dance visions the crow acts as guide for the vision-seeker to the land of the dead.[23]

The emphasis placed upon crows and magpies in the Ghost Dance painting style is not surprising in view of the specific relationships these birds had to Ghost Dance philosophy. However, the presence of some other kinds of birds in Ghost Dance art might be better explained by other factors.

The bird (as Thunderbird) played an important role in Sun Dance symbolism throughout the Plains. Images of the Thunderbird were painted onto Sun Dance center poles and replicas of eagle nests were placed in Sun Dance lodges; also, eagle feathers were placed in some Sun Dance lodges as prayers for rain and for vegetation. In the

40. Dress, deerskin, Arapaho, pre-1903.

41. *Shirt, deerskin, Kiowa, c. 1890.*

reach of the Wind River reservation in Wyoming where the Eastern Shoshone and Arapaho were living. The Bannock and Shoshone of Fort Hall were thus in a position to share knowledge of the new religion with their Arapaho neighbors. The Arapaho subsequently transmitted the ideas to the Cheyenne and the Sioux.[28] In the fall of 1889 the Sioux learned of the Ghost Dance religion,[29] and by 1890 Ghost Dance garments were made and worn by them for protection and to symbolize hope for the emergence of a new world order. Other tribes soon learned of the special outfits from the Sioux.[30]

Northern Plains, the bird played an especially important role in Sun Dance symbolism where Thunderbird eclipsed the Sun as a primary spiritual entity. Thus, it is possible to speculate that Thunderbird and/or eagle may have been added to the corpus of Ghost Dance bird symbols by people living on the Northern Plains who are said to have functioned as interpreters of the Ghost Dance to their neighbors living farther south.

The Northern Plains region was the probable point of entry of the Ghost Dance into the Plains. Bannock and Northern Shoshone people living at the Fort Hall reservation in Idaho were among the first to accept the Ghost Dance religion.[24] These groups subsequently served as conduits for the dissemination of Ghost Dance philosophies to the tribes of the Northern Plains.[25] The Bannock were of Northern Paiute stock, and, hence, spoke the same language as Wovoka, the Nevada Ghost Dance prophet; thus, transmission of ideas was facilitated. Emissaries from many Plains tribes traveled to speak with Wovoka, stopping first at Fort Hall to enlist the services of Bannock interpreters who accompanied them to Nevada.[26] The Fort Hall reserve was, therefore, well appointed socially to serve as a primary distribution center for the Ghost Dance doctrine on the Plains.

Fort Hall was also ideally situated geographically to function as the dissemination point of the Ghost Dance religion to people living on the Plains. Fort Hall's favorable position was in part due to the fact that it was located at the junction of a north-south railroad from Utah to Montana, and an east-west transcontinental line.[27] In addition, Fort Hall was situated within easy

42. *Wovoka, Ghost Dance Prophet, c. 1921.*

33

43. Feathers, golden eagle, painted, Kiowa, c. 1890.

Ghost Dance Art and the Sun Dance

In Cheyenne and Arapaho Sun Dance ceremonies observed between 1901 and 1960,[31] two performers played vital roles; The Sacred Woman was the symbolic reproducer of the tribe, the family, the buffalo, and of Creation as a whole,[32] and the Pledger was the receiver of the procreative power of the Supreme Being through the Sacred Woman, his wife. Throughout the days of the ceremony these two individuals were painted with varying combinations of a number of designs including crescents, sun discs, Morning Star (drawn as a diamond or square turned on end), lines or bands called "trails", dragonflies, sacred pipes, and forked zigzags representing lightning or power.

Four designs recurred in successive Sun Dance body painting episodes: crescent moon, Morning Star, sun disc, and trails. Choice of motifs varied according to the painting episode in question.

44. Dress, muslin, Sioux, 50/3054, c. 1890.

Either the Sun or Morning Star was painted onto the chests of the principal performers, and their faces were decorated with either a sun symbol or a Morning Star design; a crescent moon was painted onto each of their backs above the right shoulder blade. Trails were painted around their wrists, mid or upper-arms, ankles or mid-leg, and midriff. In some painting episodes, participants were painted with trails which ran from the center chest diagonally up to the shoulders, across the shoulders and down the arms; trails were also sometimes drawn down the sides of the body and the outer leg. Trails were said to signify the paths from the heart to the homes of the Four Sacred Beings who dwell at the four semi-cardinal directions of the world. For the Cheyenne, these Four Sacred Beings guarded Creation.[33]

Two obvious differences characterize Ghost Dance garment painting and Sun Dance body painting (as seen on the Arapaho and Cheyenne principal performers). These are: (1) Most Ghost Dance garments are decorated with a crescent moon painted at the center of the chest (the Sun Dancer wears the crescent moon on his or her back in flanking position); and (2) Birds are painted onto large numbers of Ghost Dance garments (but, birds were not painted onto the bodies of Sun Dance performers). Thus, three painted motifs were consistently worn by both Ghost Dancers and Sun Dancers (Arapaho and Cheyenne): crescent, star, and trails. But, Ghost Dancers also frequently painted bird motifs onto their garments, whereas Sun Dancers frequently painted sun discs onto the bodies of their principal performers (between 1901 and 1969). The parallels encourage speculation that at least a portion of Ghost Dance symbolism may have been drawn from the same iconographic reservoir as was that of the best known of all Plains world renewal ceremonies: the Sun Dance. The variations in the two symbolic systems also encourage speculation.

The Need for Future Research

The goal of this study has been to arrive at a workable definition of traits which are held in common by a large number of dresses and shirts that are collectively referred to as "Ghost shirts" or "Ghost Dance outfits." This synthesis is not intended to represent the final word on the study of Ghost Dance art. Rather, it is meant to provide a theoretical point of view which might serve as a point of departure for future analyses. Further research is needed to delineate the specifics of a number of important considerations which are not addressed here, such as the relationship of the Ghost Dance style to others extant on the Plains in the late 19th and early 20th centuries, questions relating to attribution of specific garments, and considerations regarding the identification of tribal substyles which, taken together, comprise Ghost Dance art.

It is often difficult, and sometimes it is impossible, to assign proper dates and other attributions to Ghost Dance garments which were collected at points in time after they were made or used. Even items which are accompanied by reputable collection information generally cannot guarantee authenticity as to such crucial details as date of manufacture, iconographic interpretation, artist's identity, or cultural attribution. Problems such as these leave us with many questions about Ghost Dance art which have yet to be answered. For instance, did both men and women decorate Ghost Dance garments? What role did the marketplace play in the production of Ghost Dance art during the last decade of the 19th century and thereafter? Were the majority of the Ghost Dance style garments we know of today ever worn by their makers? If so, on what occasions? Is it conceivable that a single prolific artist might be responsible for a sizable number of artworks attributed to the Ghost Dance style, and is thus largely responsible for definition of the style? Unanswered questions abound.

Another question yet to be resolved is the precise nature of the relationship between Sun Dance and Ghost Dance symbolism. Visual similarities between the two design systems lead us to speculate as to the possible existence of a historical and/or a symbolic relationship. Were the symbol systems of both drawn from a common source, or did one perhaps derive from the other? Are the similarities simply fortuitous, or is it possible that each symbol system cross-fertilized the other? It is not unlikely that the same individuals might have been involved in both the Ghost Dance and the Sun Dance, and, therefore, have had an effect on both ceremonies. In the early part of the 20th century Black Coyote, an Arapaho Ghost Dancer, led an Arapaho Sun Dance.34 Could this individual have infused post-1890 Sun Dance ceremonies with Ghost Dance symbolism? Only further research can shed light upon the answer to these questions.

One of the most intriguing issues relating to Ghost Dance art involves identification and assessment of tribal styles. Analysis of specific differences between tribal styles will undoubtedly prove to be illuminating, and will perhaps shed a brighter light on our understanding of the Ghost Dance art style than can be accomplished by any synthesis of traits. Imbedded in individual tribal styles are likely to be clues to meanings which

45. *Dress, deerskin, Arapaho, c. 1885.*

are lost in broad syntheses such as the one presented here. A brief discussion of a small number of unusually decorated Arapaho Ghost Dance garments illustrates this point.

Some Arapaho garments are decorated with motifs that are not typically found on Ghost Dance garments, but which occur in combination with one of more of the four hallmark designs described above. The atypical motifs are: pipe, a spread eagle quadruped (probably a pelt), rabbit, banded arc or rainbow, netted hoop or Medicine Hoop, turtle, bison, plants or trees (some with roots depicted), and female figures. These designs might be interpreted as referring to aspects of Arapaho Creation beliefs, combined with select details of Cheyenne world renewal symbolism, and Prairie Faw Faw religious revitalization ceremonialism.

Rabbit: According to Arapaho Creation traditions, Rabbit came forward with the plea that in the newly formed world, he be remembered eternally as a useful companion. The rabbit was deemed to be harmless and clean, yet also strong, kind and sympathetic.35 For these reasons, the rabbit was chosen to represent the name of the lodge, Rabbit Tipi, in which the Sun Dance principal performers' bodies were decorated with painted symbols, and ritual accessories for the sacred altar were prepared.36

Turtle: The turtle played a central role in the

46. Tobacco bag, Arapaho, c. 1890 (?).

Arapaho creation of the world, offering its body as a symbol of the earth, with its four legs representing the four cardinal directions.[37]

Pipe: In Arapaho world creation beliefs, a pipe is identified with the Creator, and it is the most sacred possession of the tribe.[38] throughout the Plains, pipes symbolize prayer and binding religious sanctity.

Hoop: The Medicine Hoop is one of the most sacred possessions of the Arapaho people;[39] it is decorated with incised crosses and conventionalized Thunderbirds. The hoop symbolizes the Arapaho creation of the world. At the same time, the hoop represents the sun, earth, sky, water and wind.[40] A Sacred Wheel is an accessory of the Arapaho Sun Dance altar, and a similar artifact has also been used in the Sioux Ghost Dance.[41]

Banded Arc and Plants: the pictorial proximity of banded arcs and plants on select Arapaho Ghost dance garments parallels their placement in the Sun Dance altars of the Arapaho and the Cheyenne people. The altars are constructed, in part, of bent colored twigs meant to represent the rainbow. Plants representing the necessities of life (food, firewood, and shade) are erected near the arc.[42] Painted bison skulls are other ritual accessories of Arapaho and Cheyenne Sun Dance altars.

Quadruped Pelt: The painted motif showing a quadruped with extremities outstretched might be a depiction of the Yellow Wolf Pelt, an important accessory in the Massaum, or Buffalo Dance, a Cheyenne ceremony which was performed for the purpose of bringing food to the people in times of scarcity.

Female figures and Plants with Roots: Female figures and plants (or trees) with roots exposed might refer to important symbols of Faw Faw religious ceremonialism. A cedar tree with roots exposed played a central role in ceremonies of a revitalization movement known as Wah-No-She's Dance, or the Faw Faw religion of the Prairie Otoe-Missouria people.[43] An important part of the ritual activities associated with this late 19th century religious movement involved women and men collecting a living cedar with its roots intact and installing it in the center of their ceremonial lodge along with the skulls of buffalo.

Conclusions
The Ghost Dance: Hostile Unification or Symbolic Reconciliation?

The United States military establishment viewed the Ghost Dance as a potentially dangerous unifying resistance movement, and

47. Dress, canvas flag, Southern Plains, c. 1890 (?).

proceeded with plans to arrest Sitting Bull, an important tribal leader who embraced Ghost Dance ideals. This disastrous misinterpretation of Ghost Dance objectives and philosophy by the United States Army resulted in a massacre of sick, starving and unarmed Indian women, babies, and elderly men at Wounded Knee, South Dakota, on December 29, 1890. The dreadful encounter is credited in the literature with bringing an end to open participation in the Ghost Dance by the Sioux and most other people on the Plains.[44]

It is true that the Ghost Dance of 1890 unified Indian people. However, the symbols painted onto Ghost Dance style garments offer silent testimony that Ghost Dance unity was not oriented toward hostility, but instead, toward an attempt to repair torn human relations. It would appear that participation in the movement likely constituted a communal plea for the renewal of a ruined earth and the opportunity for a suffering people to live "free from death, disease, and misery".[45]

Many of the designs and compositional arrangements of symbols painted onto Ghost Dance garments parallel those used in traditional Plains world renewal rituals such as the Massaum, the White Buffalo Ceremony, the Renewal of the Sacred Medicine Arrows, and the Sun Dance.[46] The concept of social and world renewal was a fundamental purpose of these ceremonies: "At the deepest of levels . . . these rituals restored and repaired human relations and achieved a symbolic reconciliation with the world and its many beings . . ."[47] The ceremonies thus share with the Ghost Dance doctrine the principle of socially renewed people living upon a regenerated earth. Therefore, the Ghost Dance art style can perhaps best be interpreted as a visual expression of commitment to principles of reconciliation, renewal and regeneration.

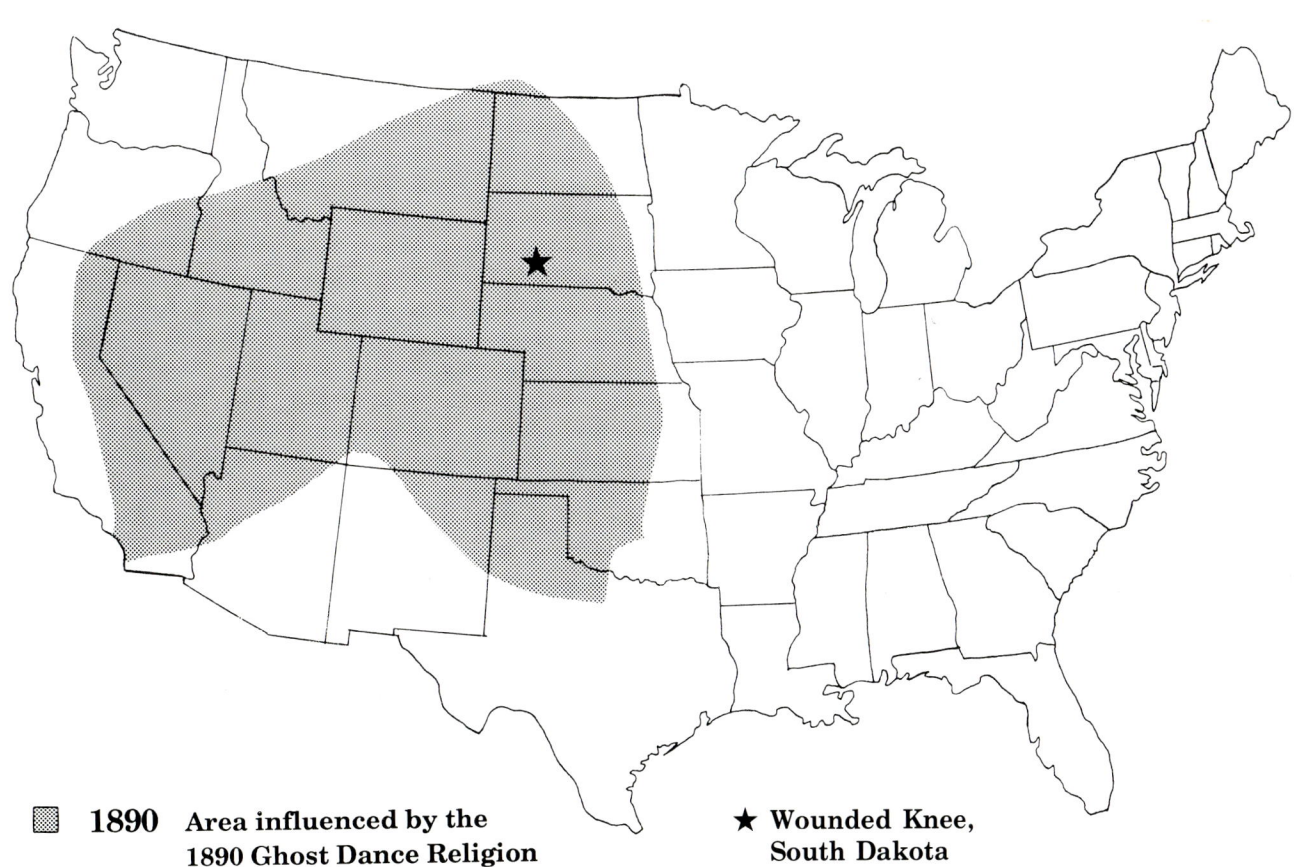

▨ **1890** Area influenced by the 1890 Ghost Dance Religion

★ Wounded Knee, South Dakota

MASSACRE AT WOUNDED KNEE, 1890: DESCENDANTS OF INDIAN SURVIVORS SPEAK

by
Jeanne Eder

The Indian side of the story of the Massacre at Wounded Knee is part of the oral traditions of the Dakota people. The oral traditions consist of the handing down by word of mouth from generation to generation those stories about people and important historic events. As part of this oral tradition many Indian tribes used "winter counts" to keep track of their tribal histories. These winter counts consisted of hides that were painted with pictures of some specific annual event that influenced the tribe for that year. Alfonso Ortiz has said: " . . . we must develop more respect within the historical profession for oral traditions, for there is much to be gained from tribes' own accounts . . ."[1]

It is thought by scholarly historians that spoken accounts handed down from generation to generation may not be as accurate as those that have been documented through the written word. Yet why is it that Indian people, as well as other cultures in the world, cling to their oral traditions? Scott Momaday, Pulitzer Prize winning Kiowa novelist has said: "The oral tradition is that process by which the myths, legends, tales, and lore of a people are formulated, communicated, and preserved in language by word of mouth, as opposed to writing."[2]

John Tosh, noted historian, has said that oral sources of study can really be divided into two categories; one of these is oral reminiscence. These are the first-hand recollections of people about a specific event, and it would be these interviews that he calls oral history. The second category is that of narratives and descriptions of people and events of the past that have been handed down by word of mouth through several generations, and these would be called oral traditions. Therefore, Tosh states: "Oral tradition may be defined as a body of knowledge which has been transmitted orally over several generations and is the collective property of the members of a given society."[3]

For many cultures of the world, oral traditions validate ethnic identity, social status and rights to ancestral lands. This differs from Western society in which such validation is achieved through the use of written documents. Taking this a step further, Tosh suggests that the oral traditions are a means to teach the values and beliefs that are important to a culture. They can also be used to validate political and social arrangements that currently exist. In the case of the Massacre at Wounded Knee, one needs to understand the oral traditions of the Dakota people in order to understand the current political and social perspective of the non-Indian culture that the Dakota people may have today.

One of the perspectives that Dakota people had, and still have, is a fear of reprisals for elaborating on their oral traditions as they relate to a specific event such as the Massacre at Wounded Knee. In the interviews with the descendants of survivors that were collected it is apparent that there is some reluctance to elaborate on details of the massacre. Jessie Kills Close to the Lodge Crow said: "There are things that books tell but are not true. I guess Indian peoples were scared to tell."[4] Calvin Jumping Bull said: "We have many, many oral traditions about Wounded Knee. . . . People know they have relatives that survived but sometimes they are reluctant, or refuse to give information. But I think that in order for people, the outside world, to know exactly what happened; people say it was a Battle, but it was not that at all. So they have to know the truth."[5]

48. *Claudia Iron Hawk Sully, president, Wounded Knee Survivors Association. Wounded Knee, South Dakota, 1990.*

Claudia Iron Hawk Sully is a descendant of a survivor. Her father's mother was Comes Crawling and she was one of the women who got away. In her interview Claudia said: "My father told me . . . every little noise she hears, banging noise she'll jump. And she has fear in her all the time. Like when some white people come to take stories or talk to my grandpa about Little Big Horn. They said she used to hide. She didn't want to be around. She had a fear of white people for a long time."[6]

This kind of fear has created a silence that has lasted for one hundred years. It is not unlike other silences observed by other survivors in similar situations. Each survivor has been a witness and each must decide for himself or herself how to speak of the event or not speak of the event. The question is: In speaking will one bring greater hardship on one's own people? For in the speaking there will be a fear of retaliation. And yet in trying to speak of this event, there are no words to totally describe it. Nonetheless, many survivors feel that they have a duty to speak in order to give meaning to their own life.

Where do we begin to tell this story of the events that led up to the Massacre at Wounded Knee? Students of Indian History must first grasp the perspective that Indian nations were sovereign nations and negotiated the sale of their lands on that basis. As sovereign nations they were, and still are treated as equals by the United States. They negotiated treaties which are legally binding contracts between sovereign nations and represent the Supreme Law of the land. In the five hundred years of living with the invading white man, the sovereignty of Indian nations has become more limited, yet they still adhere to their belief that they are sovereign entities. Many recent court decisions support that claim.

Under the auspices of "Manifest Destiny" the United States government planned the invasion and takeover of lands belonging to Indian nations, and that included the Sioux lands which we are dealing with in this event. Beginning with the Expedition of Lewis and Clark, the value of Indian lands was to be scrutinized and documented for future use and exploitation by whites. If the Sioux leaders could have fathomed the kinds of scientific studies that were being conducted on the Plains, they would have had a clearer understanding of the motives and direction of the Europeans' invasion. The design was to open up the west to white settlers and to confine the Indians to reserved lands and promote civilization among them.

The first in a series of treaties was signed in 1851 at Fort Laramie. The objectives of this treaty were for peace and to allow the United States to open up roads and establish military posts in Indian territory. The treaty also forced tribes into identifying specific tribal boundaries. With this treaty various exploratory visits could be made by the military. Tribes then could be approached individually by the United States forces and enticed into giving up their lands. It was the old "divide and conquer" scheme. Numerous forces were at work to push Indian nations into giving up their property.

49. *Villa of Brule, 1891.*

One early government geological exploration of the region was made by Lieutenant G. K. Warren, United States Army. He reported to the War Department about his expedition into the Black Hills under the title of Explorations in Nebraska and Dakota in the Years 1855, 1856, and 1857. Warren said: "The Blackhills . . . contain an inexhaustible quantity of the finest timber, mostly pine . . . I will, however, propose a plan for obtaining this timber and rendering it useful to future settlers."[7]

Even newspapers accounts of the day, especially after the discovery of gold on Indian lands was verified, were enticing people to Indian lands. The Weekly Missoulian, on September 2, 1874, gave this account of General Custer's report of the Black Hills: ". . . no portion of the country can boast of richer or better pasturage, purer water . . . and of greater natural advantage to the farmer or stock raiser than are to be found in the Black Hills. . . . "The Sioux would inevitably have to challenge the appearance of these invading forces on their ancestral lands.

Another aspect of all this is the significant difference between a treaty signing group of Indians versus a non-treaty signing group. There are still people who feel that their ancestors never signed a treaty giving away the ancestral lands of the Sioux Nation. The 1851 Fort Laramie Treaty was followed by the 1868 Fort Laramie Treaty, after Chief Red Cloud successfully forced the United States to abandon its military forts along the Bozeman trail. He also agreed to new boundaries and to settle within those boundaries. The 1868 treaty would also stipulate that no future treaties would be signed unless three-fourths of all adult Sioux males signed the agreement. In an Agreement of 1876, the Blackhills would be ceded by the Sioux, but the agreement was not fully signed by three-fourths of all adult Sioux males. The failure of the United States to comply with the 1868 Treaty led to a long-standing suit brought to the Supreme Court by the Sioux against the government for the illegal taking of the Black Hills. According to Robert Utley: "In none of the treaty councils were the chiefs fully informed of the contents of the documents they were asked to sign. Treaty commissioners made much of the rations and other gifts that were promised but said little if anything about the land and freedom the Indians would be expected to surrender . . . Repeatedly victimized, it is not surprising that the Sioux brought to all subsequent councils a profound distrust of the whiteman . . . ."[8]

Red Cloud visited the President in Washington, D.C. to say: "I was born at the Forks of the Platte and I was told that the land belonged to me. From N.E.S.W. the red men have come to to the Great Father's house. These Oglallas are the last who come here but I came here to hear and listen to the Great Father's words. They have promised me traders, but we have none . . . When you send goods to me they would steal all along the road so when it reaches me it was only a handful. They hold a paper for me to sign and that is all I get for my goods. I know now the people you sent out there are all liars . . . Look at me, I am poor and naked. I do not want war with my government. . . ."[9]

Thus there are those individuals who believe that their ancestors never signed away their ancestral lands, and they carry a certain distrust of the systems that did not meet any of the promised treaty rights. This means that there can be internal strife among the Sioux that carries over into today's legal activities. That is something to keep in mind as the events of the Massacre at Wounded Knee unfold.

December 29, 1890, was a sad day for the Dakota people. It was a day that would live in the memory of the Indian people everywhere. It was the day that Big Foot's band of Minniconju were massacred. This is a story of the descendants of some of those survivors. It is their story and where possible their words are used. Please keep in mind that these are taken from spoken accounts and that their command of the English language varies. At times cultural differences are prevalent. The following represents a selection of material taken from interviews of descendants of survivors of the Massacre at Wounded Knee, South Dakota. The interviews concentrated on how particular individuals survived and what they experienced. Many of those interviewed were telling what their fathers and grandfathers and grandmothers had told them. Thus, some of the quotes are contained within other quotes.

Despite the fact that most historians feel that the Massacre at Wounded Knee was the result of the Ghost Dance craze that swept through the Sioux people, many of those interviewed were not involved in the Ghost Dance movement, and many were not members of Big Foot's Band. An interview with Leonard Little Finger talking about his grandfather verified this when he said: "They were all young boys and they were out riding that day when Big Foot came through, and there was a large band of people, he said they were travelling slowly so '. . . we just went over and join in with them and we knew some of the people so we rode horseback with them and pretty soon it was evening.' There was nothing planned, there was no, as some of the books say, they were planning a Ghost Dance, they were gonna unite

50. *Shield, Arapaho, c. 1890.*

and enter into battle, all these sorts of things. It was a group of boys that were out, just fate had it that they would end up with them and spend the rest of their lives down there."[10]

Chief Eagle was told by his grandfather that there were Oglallas, Rosebud, Cheyenne and Arapaho Indians who were holding a Ghost Dance at a place called the Strong Hold. They left the Strong Hold when cold, sickness and hunger forced them to join up with Big Foot's group. This also verifies that Big Foot's band was not actively participating in a Ghost Dance at the time. According to Chief Eagle: " . . . they were surrounded by U.S. Cavalry and taken to Owichn Kte (Wounded Knee Creek) . . . They say it was the cavalry revenge over Custer's Battle."[11]

This is not to say, however, that the Ghost Dance religion was not significant and that there were not individuals in Big Foot's camp who would have been active members of the Ghost Dance religion. As the Sioux were confined more and more to a smaller land base, the next step in the assimilationist movement by the invading white man was to attack the traditional Sioux religion. In 1883, as part of a massive campaign to "Civilize and Christianize" the Indians, the Commissioner of Indian Affairs distributed a set of rules to stamp out the Indian religion. Each Indian agent received instructions to organize a Court of Indian Offenses to enforce the rules, which included the banning of the Sun Dance religion, feasting, and dancing. The Indian agent could enforce penalties of fines, imprisonment, hard labor, or withhold rations.[12]

When a people are in trouble, they will turn to religion to search for meaning and direction in their lives. With their traditional religion banned and their medicine men dying, the Sioux were no different in embracing the new Ghost Dance religion that promised the regeneration of the earth and the return of deceased ancestors and the buffalo. It is interesting to note that the Ghost Dance religion was rooted in Christianity. Also keep in mind that this promise of the return of ancestors and buffalo is a view developed by non-Indian ethnohistorians and anthropologists. So their views may not be as accurate when taken from the Indian view.

The new prophet of the religion was a Paiute sheepherder named Wovoka. His father died and he was adopted by a white family who changed his name to Jack Wilson. While with this family he was steeped in their Christian religion. He also encountered the Mormon religion and later was to work in the Puget Sound region where he was influenced by the Shaker religion. The Shaker religion utilized the trance as a part of its ceremonies. According to Utley, "Wovoka learned the doctrine, participated in some of its rituals, and observed its regenerating effect upon converts."[13] Wovoka's own rise as a Messiah began during the eclipse of the sun. Wovoka had been very ill and during the eclipse he had a vision in which he viewed heaven and spoke with God. There God showed him a world free of white people. Wovoka told his followers that a signal would be given to the Indians when this was going to happen. The ground would shake and they were to fasten sacred feathers in their hair and they would be lifted to the sky while the new land covered the old. The new land would then push all the white people back across the ocean. When this shaking of the earth was over, the Indians would return to earth to find their deceased families and friends and life restored. From that point on they would enjoy eternal life. By praying, dancing and singing the Ghost dance songs they could make brief visits to view this new world for themselves.[14]

Francis He Crow is directly related to Big Foot. He is the great-great-grandson of Big Foot. He Crow was killed at Wounded Knee and was the son of Big Foot. He Crow's son was Jackson He Crow and he was a child survivor of Wounded Knee. Jackson He Crow's son was Moses He Crow, who in turn was the father of Francis. In the interview with Francis He Crow, one begins to get a better understanding of the Ghost Dance itself. He talked about how some Sioux men travelled for forty-six days to reach the Paiute Reservation and there received instruction in the

51. *Tobacco bag, Arapaho, c. 1880.*

Ghost Dance religion. One of the things that they had to do was to climb a mountain. He said: ". . . before they climb that mountain, they all line up and each one they have a praying sticks, arrows . . . shirts and shawls. They are sacred objects. So they climb that mountain and when they get to the top they say there are a lot of black rocks up there. All sit in a big circle. One got up and he prayed. And when he was through, they see this sign as a cloud and a grave marker. And there is a white man standing there with his head down. And he put his head up and he talked to these Indians . . . It was Jesus. They saw Jesus. And now he is showing them the crucifixion. This is how they kill . . . this is what they have done to me. He cries. . . . This white man talked to them and said, what you see and how they arrest me . . . you see everything. They asked him to adopt the white religion because the Indian religion is not going to last. It is going to dissolve."[15] It is obvious in this case that the individual has given us a look at how the Christian concepts of the resurrection of Jesus have been incorporated into the belief system of the Indian people. I ask the reader to consider this: Why wouldn't a better religion evolve? The traditional Indian religions were under attack and Christianity was being forced upon the Indians. How else could they hope to survive in such desperate conditions, except by taking this new religion, incorporating it into their own, and expanding it to make it better than the white man's religion?

From this point on, the Sioux began to amass several grievances that would contribute to their easy acceptance of the new religion. Their rations were cut because of fatal epidemics among the young and the old alike; drought created hunger; and boundary disputes created problems between reservations. Many of the bands of Sioux were ripe for the introduction of a new Messiah. This made many of the Indian agents nervous.

During this time in the history of the Plains Indian, the Indian Agent played a significant and oftentimes destructive role in the social and cultural changes instituted on the Indian reservations. In a time when Indian Agents were forcibly influencing social and administrative decisions on Indian reservations, Pine Ridge was handicapped by the appointment of Daniel F. Royer, physician, pharmacist and the local politician. Utley said this of Royer: ". . . one of the worst specimens ever produced by the spoils system, was weak, excitable, and easily panicked, so much so that the Sioux named him 'Young-Man-Afraid-of-Indians.' He quickly made himself a target of contempt and ridicule, and he proved utterly wanting in any ability to stem the drift of anarchy.

Repeatedly he ordered the dancers to stop dancing and return to their cabins, but they simply laughed at him. Repeatedly he bombarded his superiors with frantic appeals for soldiers."[16] These appeals would eventually be heeded.

Utley's book, The Indian Frontier, gives the briefest account of the event prior to the massacre. He said that the appearance of troops at Pine Ridge only seemed to unite the Ghost Dancers in defense of their religion. He divides the Sioux at Pine Ridge into "friendlies" and "hostiles." Those who were not hostile and who did not embrace the new religion with open enthusiasm gathered at the agency. The "hostiles," some three thousand of them led by Short Bull and Kicking Bear, took up position in a place called the "Stronghold." This was an elevated tableland in the remote northwestern corner of the reservation. Alex White Plume's account says that there had been a Ghost Dance thirteen miles west of Bridger and: ". . . they broke up and left and they were heading up for Sitting Bull's camp then some of Sitting Bull's brothers, after Sitting Bull was killed, came down and met up with them and some of the survivors from Sitting Bull's band were with them so they joined up with Big Foot's band . . . ."[17]

In the meantime, General Crook had died and this left Major General Nelson A. Miles in command of the military in South Dakota. Miles' attempt to avoid violence with those in the Stronghold was thwarted by two things. The first was the killing of Sitting Bull. Vine Deloria notes: "In early December of 1890 the government, fearful of the Ghost Dance—which was spreading throughout the West from its place of origin in Nevada—arranged to assassinate Sitting Bull, the Hunkpapa holy man of the Standing Rock Sioux Reservation, when it learned that he too had embraced the new religion."[18] As a result of Sitting Bull's death, many of his people fled to Big Foot's camp. Of course, the agency then sent out word that they must all report to the agency at Pine Ridge. If they did not then the military would be sent after them. The second thing that would thwart Miles' intentions was the Massacre at Wounded Knee.

Big Foot had embraced the Ghost Dance religion just long enough to get his name on the list of trouble makers that was put together by the various Indian agents. In actuality, Red Cloud had invited him to Pine Ridge to help him end any troubles with the "friendlies." So when Big Foot and his people were joined by the refugees from Sitting Bull's band they knew that they had to head for Pine Ridge. They did so hoping that they could receive protection from Red Cloud. So, in the middle of winter, the people of Big Foot's Band decided to make the journey to Pine Ridge. With few weapons and little clothing, they moved south through the Badlands hoping to make it to safety with Red Cloud.

Lawson Iron Hawk said: "My grandfather told me that the Indian people were coming to Red Cloud Agency from the north . . . for the winter . . . chief Big Foot was sick, he was sick with pneumonia, so he rode up ahead in a blanket. They had a white flag put on the wagon and as they got to the end of the Badlands he said that they were intercepted, and they were surrounded by soldiers at the place of the Badlands. Some say it was north near Manderson. And some say it was probably up there by Cedar Pass. Anyway, they were surrounded by soldiers at gun point."[19]

Iron Hawk's grandmother on his father's side was Comes Crawling who was a survivor. She told him: ". . . it was a hard walk. Some of them wrapped their feet in gunny sacks and skins. There weren't no overshoes in those days. . . ."[20]

Calvin Jumping Bull said: ". . . Big Foot, the leader of the group, he came down from up North, he's a Minniconju . . . he knows how to talk to the people and unite people and when he came down, he also came down with some of Sitting Bull's people on December 15, 1890 . . . Big Foot had, I guess, pneumonia and he wasn't really able to ride a horse or even walk with being bed ridden. . . ."[21]

Chief Eagle stated in his interview that: ". . . they were surrounded by U.S. Cavalry and taken to Owichn Kte (Wounded Knee Creek) below Porcupine Butte. They say it was cavalry's revenge over Custer's Battle. A group of A Ki Chi Ta (Dog Soldiers) heard about the government intention of killing the Indians, so they formed to help the Indians, but it happened too fast."[22]

In his book, The Long Death, Ralph K. Andrist says that one of the main concerns was that the Indians had to be disarmed. So: "At about eight o'clock the warriors came out of their lodges and

52. *Famous Battery E, Wounded Knee.*

sat on the ground in a semicircle. . . . Troops stationed by the council ring were ordered to move up to within ten yards of the seated warriors, and other enlisted men were detailed to search the tepees. . . ."[23] As the searching went on, tensions rose and Utley's description in The Indian Frontier of the American West, 1846-1890 gives us a clear insight into the beginning of the massacre: "A medicine man pranced about inciting the men to fight; their Ghost Shirts would protect them, he said. Nervous troopers fingered their carbine triggers. One seized a deaf man and grasped his rifle. It went off. The chanting priest threw a handful of dirt into the air. . . ."[24]

One particular interview gives validity to the Ghost Dance shirts that were worn. Rachel Afraid of Enemy Hollow Horn said: ". . . my children are the fourth generation of Wounded Knee survivors. At the time of the massacre my grandfather was in it. He had nine bullet holes in his gold shirt. He died [in 1932] from the wounds from the Wounded Knee massacre. His name was Solomon Afraid of Enemy."[25]

From the Indian perspective of the events preceding the shooting spree, Calvin Jumping Bull related this information: "Big Foot . . . He told his people not to cause any trouble . . . after the soldiers decided to disarm the group, one of the young men, a man by the name of Black Coyote, he's suppose to be a deaf mute and he refused to give up his gun and I guess by struggling over the soldiers tried to take the gun away from him the gun went off and that's the start."[26]

Lawson Iron Hawk's grandmother, Comes Crawling, told this story: "In the morning they called out all the people to assemble in the middle . . . She said a soldier yelled something and that here, soldiers started coming into camp. And they started ransacking all their belongings. And they picked up guns, knives, bow and arrows, axes, hatchets, even awls used for sewing. And they were all piled in the middle and it was cold that morning she says. They noticed that all around them were soldiers and the children, the kids started crying because they were afraid. Some of them soldiers got down in kneeling position and they all loaded up their guns . . . and there were

53. Colt Model 1873, Single Action Revolver, .45 caliber.

some hotchkiss guns up ahead and they loaded those up too . . . when the soldiers got through searching and finding all of those, anything they would consider a weapons, an Indian man, an old man, he started to sing. The man kneeled and said 'Something is going to happen to us.' This old man, he started to sing a death song . . . They disarmed them and then shot and killed them. Old Men, old people, women and children and even babies."[27]

Phoebe Iron Hawk spoke of her aunt's husband, Frank Sits Poor, as a survivor. "He was eight years old then and his family was all there with him when this happened . . . He told us that the ones that were camped there didn't have no weapon. They didn't have no weapon, gun or anything. So they made them all stand in a row. They put them all in a row to see if they can talk about what's going on but as they stood over them there, I guess, one of the elders got tired of standing up. So he had a cane inside of his blanket. So just as he was going to put that to stand up again . . . that's when they thought he had a gun and they all start shooting from up on the hills."[28]

Utley further explains the massacre: "In a murderous melee at close range, soldiers and Indians shot, stabbed, and clubbed one another. Weakly Big Foot rose from his pallet to watch. A volley killed him and most of the headmen lined up behind him. Abruptly the two sides separated, and from the hill the artillery went into action. Exploding shells flattened the Sioux tipis and filled the air with deadly shrapnel. In less than an hour most of the fighting had ended. . . . Nearly two-thirds of Big Foot's band had been cut down, at least 150 dead and 50 wounded, and

54. Sword and Scabbard, c. 1864.

55. *Bird's-eye view of the Canyon at Wounded Knee, 1891.*

perhaps more who were never reported. The army lost 25 dead and 39 wounded."[29]

Yet there were survivors despite the mass confusion. Utley says that the Indian village ". . . boiled with panic stricken women and children." 30 When the artillery fire ended the soldiers hunted down those survivors that they could find in the ravine and shot them. Andrist stresses that when the shooting stopped, a line of bodies extended for about two miles.

Iron Hawk's grandmother was one of the survivors who got away: "My grandmother was wounded . . . Some of them pretended they were dead . . . Some men which were wounded, the soldiers came along and shot them again, probably to make sure they were dead . . . She pretended she was dead. So they passed them up. There was a draw, a dry draw which some of those Indian ran in the draw. These soldiers, there was so many of them that some were caught in these corners, and stood there above them and shot them there."[31]

Another survivor was Good Crow, a medicine man. His story was told by his grandson Steven Good Crow, Steven's mother was Frances White Lance and her father was Good Crow. Steven said: "My grandfather laid in the bushes and smoke was all over, his feet was bleeding, but the soldiers didn't see him. He said later a coyote came to him. He told him to get up and walk, he walked to a house and then to Rosebud."[32]

Calvin Jumping Bull talked about his grandfather, Peter Stands, who was about eight years old at the time and survived to tell his story: "He claimed that he was a young boy maybe around eight years old, but he was wounded, but he got away and as a young man, I guess, the only way he could get around was on crutches, cause you know the wound healed by itself . . . so he couldn't use the leg . . . later on in life he used a wheel chair."[33]

Phoebe Iron Hawk had this to say about Frank Sits Poor: ". . . he did escape from them when they all start shooting because he was a boy. So he ran in one of those gullies and start running this way towards Manderson, and he hid out in a cave for a while. Watching what was going on. So they had all those horses, their legs were shot out and were broken. Some were running here and there while he was sitting there waiting. So he escaped from there and walked all the way to Grass Creek . . . but his mom and others, they all died right there."[34]

Adolph Hollow Horn's wife was Grace Hollow Horn. Her grandfather was Afraid of Enemy and was a survivor. Yet one of his children was killed at Wounded Knee. The shawl his daughter had been wearing had a bullet hole through it. Now one of the descendants carries the name Tashina Opi (Wounded Shawl).

Leonard Little Finger gave a very descriptive account of his grandfather's recollection of the shooting: "He said that when the firing started it was one bang, and it was just like this, smoke and dust and he said, 'I looked off to the side and a ravine was there so I ran for the ravine. There was a lot of us running, and just before I got to the edge of the ravine, that's when they hit me from the back and I rolled. I felt a sharp jab of pain. I knew that I was shot. When I got up to run, I could still run so I took about four steps and I got hit again, same leg, and this time I could feel my shoe go.' He said he had some boots on and he could feel that whole thing slide off. At that point he said: 'I knew I had to get away. As I looked up that ravine, there was about five or six of them running so I just ran as fast as I could. I caught up to them and we went up and behind us, the solders got to the ravine and they started to fire down because there was a lot of people in there. So we continued and we got up on top. We were a long ways from where we were originally but in that whole ravine, there was people here and there and soldiers were all down upon them. The firing stopped and we laid there and we heard this scout, he called out in Lakota. He said, 'There will be no more shooting. All of you that are in the ravine come on out and we will help you.' So there was people laying alongside the ravine. They would only get as far as the level ground and you could start seeing people coming up. They were coming up over the ravine and as they come up, the soldiers were standing there watching them and when they got up to the top, there was one shot like that again. A lot of people got killed then. You could just see them fall and we laid there and watched.'"[35]

56. *Doll, Sioux, c. 1890.*

57. *Burial of the (Indian) dead at Wounded Knee, January 1, 1891.*

"'The last thing that I saw was the firing had ended and the soldiers were going around and they were kicking people. They kicked them and if they moved, they'd shoot them. This woman was sitting on the ground and she had a baby in her arms and she was rocking it. You could see the rocking. This soldier came up and he grabbed that bundle from her and when he grabbed it, she went to get it, but he got the baby and he threw the baby on the ground. I seen him take that pistol and he fired two shots into that bundle. That woman got up crying and started to run for the baby, and the soldier took that pistol and as she came by he hit her on the back of the head and knocked her down. He took his boot and put it on her throat. He put that on her throat and he fired about four times. At that point, that's all I could take and we left from there. We didn't know where we was at, which way we were going, but we were heading off in the direction of west.'"³⁶

Little Finger's story is a little longer than some of the others. He was one of the original group of young men who just happened to join in with Big Foot's Band and were not involved other than having some relatives in the band. He goes on to explain his journey: "That evening, overnight we laid someplace. The next day we got down to the Mission and there was a priest there and he gave me some powder and he said to put it on my leg and he bandaged it up. I was okay and the others were okay and they told us that we better leave. They didn't want us there. They said that there was gonna be come more shooting so we left. We didn't know which way to got but we thought we'd head back north, so we followed this canyon . . . we stayed there all winter . . . its a stronghold, in a sense, because you've got that deep canyon in the front and then there's a ridge up on top."³⁷ Little Finger and his group of friends would use the top of that ridge to scout out the territory. Leonard Little Finger said that his grandfather could see people all around down there and on many occasions they saw the soldiers going back and forth. They knew they were looking for them. When the spring came they went down and that is when he met Leonard's grandmother. Before meeting Leonard's grandmother, Little Finger was called Yellow Horse and she broke his little finger and it was to remain crooked forever. So when they were allotting land, he changed his name to Sha-shte (Little Finger). Leonard Little Finger says that: "They all settled in this area, He Crow, Pipe on Head, Blind Man, Good Voice Flute, Stands. He said there was six or seven of them here and from that point on they lived here. They never went back, but two years later, Buffalo Bill came to Pine Ridge and they were recruiting some dancers to go to Europe . . . He was eighteen at that time."[38]

According to Vine Deloria, "The wounded were left to die in a three-day blizzard, and the United States handed out over twenty Congressional Medals of Honor to soldiers of the Seventh Cavalry who had participated in the massacre."[39] The dead of Big Foot's people were buried in a mass grave described by Utley: "Some whites stripped part of the corpses for Ghost Shirts and other mementos of the occasion. Then still frozen stiff, the bodies were dumped unceremoniously into the hole . . . When the last body had been rolled into the grave, the whites lined up around it and had their picture taken. Then they shoveled dirt into the pit and rode back to the agency."[40]

Bernice Eagle Hawk White Hawk, from Manderson, South Dakota, gives a good description of her family's work to aid the wounded and dying survivors. Her mother's name was Ruth Plenty Wounds and Bernice's grandmother was Rattling Wounds. All of the family had been Ghost Dancing and one of Ruth's uncles came and told them to pack up their things and leave. According to Bernice: "He said they might come over and kill you guys next. So my grandmother go get the horses . . . My grandmother has some chickens . . . but she has to chase those chickens all over first. They got them in the wagon . . .

59. Monument at the Mass Grave, Wounded Knee Cemetery.

and then left towards Gajaw, was cut across to Pine Ridge. So they went that way . . . to that Catholic Hall and they stayed there. And they brought wounded people. I don't know how many but she said they brought them back on the wagon and they all cold and sick. Got pneumonia. Maybe they're breathing. So they . . . fixed beds for them, the Catholic people."[41]

In 1903 the Indians erected a monument at the site of the mass grave with an inscription that reads:

This monument is erected by surviving relatives and other Ogalalla and Cheyenne River Sioux Indians in memory of the Chief Big Foot Massacre Dec. 29, 1890. Col. Forsyth in command of U.S. Troops. Big Foot was a great chief of the Sioux Indians. He often said, "I will stand in peace till my last day comes." He did many good and brave deeds for the whiteman and the red man. Many innocent women and children who knew no wrong died here.[42]

For some of the descendants, to remember their grandparents is to remember such things as this recollection of Leonard Little Finger's: ". . . the thing I most vividly remember is sitting along the dam down here. He was getting up in years. He walked with a limp and he still rode horseback up until he died . . . he said: 'I want to tell you a story about this. I walk with a limp. I have a limp and I'm going to show you this.' He pulled his pant leg up and there was a big splash scar.

58. Leaders of the Hostiles, Pine Ridge Agency, January 1891.

60. *The Mass Grave, Wounded Knee Cemetery.*

You could see where the smooth skin reached out. It looked like it was jagged. He took his shoe off and showed me a portion of the heel that was missing. He said, 'These are scars that I have. When I was a boy, I lived in Cherry Creek. I got into a group that came down here. . . an army, they shot at us and many were killed.'"[43]

Clement C. High Hawk of Cherry Creek, South Dakota, had taken a trip with his grandfather. "I remember back in 1964, I drove for my lala, Jim High Hawk, to Pine Ridge, South Dakota. He told me about the Massacre that took place at Wounded Knee in 1890. He shed tears. He said that the U.S. Government owes us lots of money. He said I will never see the money. Then lala died in 1965."[44]

The massacre at Wounded Knee must be remembered. Karl Jaspers, a German Philosopher has said: "What men do today becomes the source of their future actions. Therefore we must know."[45] The struggle of Indian peoples in this country has been marked by an assault every twenty years. At the one-hundred-year marking of this massacre, we, as American people, must take time to remember. We are approaching another twenty year mark that if history is correct, it will dictate another harsh blow against the rights of Indian people.

The descendants of the survivors of the Massacre at Wounded Knee have taken several different approaches to marking that day. There are those like Raymond Pipe on Head who says: ". . . my father and relatives use to go to Wounded Knee mass grave for meetings and also to put flowers on the grave."[46] There are those who remember the day in their own way, whether it is with a visit to the mass grave, or a small token of flowers.

Claudia Iron Hawk Sully said that since 1907 there has been a group that has called themselves The Survivors. They have gathered together and through donations erected a monument on the site. She talked about how some of the survivors tried to gain compensation from the federal government. ". . . a lot of the people that go there were wounded. They had wounds and some of them were suffering. They had pains, but they used to go there, and then on the last day they put flowers on the grave and have an Indian traditional ceremony . . . they call themselves the Big Foot Claims at that time."[47]

This particular group is still attempting to get a

bill passed to compensate the Sioux as a means of healing their wounds. In April of 1920 an aged and retired Lieutenant General Nelson A. Miles accompanied a delegation of Pine Ridge Sioux to the office of the Commissioner of Indian Affairs in Washington, D.C. He was there to ask that compensation be given to the heirs of the victims of the Massacre at Wounded Knee. For twenty years this went before Congressional committees and never was acted upon. Today those descendants still hope for some action.[48]

Another group that has been created is the Big Foot Memorial Riders. Eugene White Hawk spoke of this group that began its ride in 1986. "I would like to experience what they went through 100 years ago . . . We decided to start on the same day they left from Bridger, take the same routes, camp at the same camp sites, travel the same times of day. . . ."[49] He said that the first year there were fifteen riders and they experienced the cold days and the lack of food and water. Several of them fasted during the ride. As they approached Wounded Knee that last day, White Hawk said: "We usually take and carry that white flag on the last day. To some people that white flag, they think that we're giving up, but that's not the reason why we are carrying that white flag. The white flag to us is hope for peace throughout the world, that there will be no more wars."[50]

Tex Broken Nose has said: "I came to the Strong Hold along with my two sons, one of my sons rode three years ago. We are from the Big Foot clan. My wife's great-grandfather; she is from Pipe on Head. We hope that our participation here each year will be a lesson to the Army. We never will forget what happen to the innocent women, children and men at Wounded Knee, after they took all their weapons away."[51]

Daniel Afraid of Hawk is a descendant of Afraid of Hawk who was a survivor of the Wounded Knee Massacre. He said: "Our people died in a pitiful way at Wounded Knee, (Muka si na Kiyupi) buried under the mother earth. Here is a song in remembrance of them, also prayers."[52]

Orval Looking Horse, Keeper of the Sacred White Buffalo Calf Pipe is from Green Grass, South Dakota. He said: "I ride with the staff, with the Big Foot Memorial Ride from Bridger, South Dakota, to Wounded Knee in memory of our ancestors, Chief Big Foot and his band who were killed here. As we travel the cold, we fast, pray for the sick, the elders, the children, and the Indians behind the bars in prisons."[53]

61. *Proud Young Rider Holding Photograph of Riders. Pine Ridge Reservation.*

The Big Foot Memorial Riders event has increased steadily. In its third year they numbered between seventy and eighty riders and they are hoping that in December of 1990, the number will go even higher. They say that this year, the one hundredth anniversary of the Massacre at Wounded Knee will be their last year, but they aren't sure what will really happen after 1990.

For the sake of Indian people everywhere, the memories of these survivors must not be forgotten or lost. Elie Wiesel who has devoted his life to anti-descrimination, has said: "What do we do with our memories? We must deal with them or they will crush us . . . Those who have died in anonymity must be remembered in anonymity. Our collective remembrance must save future generations from anonymity."[54] With this in mind, may we remember those massacred at Wounded Knee Creek in 1890 and may we never repeat that same kind of oppression.

62. *Wounded Knee Site Today.*

BIBLIOGRAPHIES AND NOTES

WOUNDED KNEE: A HISTORY
Alvin M. Josephy, Jr.

SELECTED BIBLIOGRAPHY

Baily, Paul, *Wovoka, the Indian Messiah.* Los Angeles: Westernlore Press, Los Angeles, 1957.

McGregor, James H., *The Wounded Knee Massacre from Viewpoint of the Sioux.* Baltimore: Wirth Brothers, 1965.

Mooney, James, *The Ghost-Dance Religion and the Sioux Outbreak of 1890.* 14th Annual Report of the Bureau of American Ethnology, 1892-93, Pt. II. Washington, 1896.

Smith, Rex Alan, *Moon of Popping Trees.* New York: Thomas Y. Crowell Co., New York, 1975.

U.S. Senate, *Wounded Knee Massacre.* Hearings Before the Committee on the Judiciary, 94th Congress, 2d Session, February 5 and 6, 1976.

Utley, Robert M., *The Last Days of the Sioux Nation.* New Haven: Yale University Press, 1963.

CRISIS AND CREATIVITY: THE GHOST DANCE ART STYLE
Trudy Thomas

NOTES

1. James Mooney, *The Ghost Dance Religion and the Sioux Outbreak of 1890,* abridged, with an introduction by Anthony F.C. Wallace (Chicago: University of Chicago Press, 1965), 19. [Originally published as Part 2 of the *14th Annual Report of the Bureau of American Ethnology,* 1892-1893, Washington, D.C.: 1896.]
2. Richard A. Pohrt, "The Indian and the American Flag," *American Indian Art Magazine* 1, no. 2 (Spring 1976): 42-48.
3. Howard D. Rodee, "The Stylistic Development of Plains Indian Painting and Its Relationship to Ledger Drawings," *Plains Anthropologist* 10, no. 30 (November 1965).
4. Robert H. Lowie, *The Assiniboin,* Anthropological Papers of the American Museum of Natural History, vol. 4 (New York: American Museum of Natural History, 1909), 1-169.
5. Clark Wissler, *Sun Dance of the Plains Indians,* Anthropological Papers of the American Museum of Natural History, vol. 16 (New York: American Museum of Natural History, 1921), 303.
6. Alice C. Fletcher and Francis La Fleche, *The Omaha Tribe,* 27th Annual Report of the Bureau of American Ethnology (Washington, D.C.: GPO, 1911), 15-675.
7. Von Del Chamberlain, *When Stars Came Down to Earth: Cosmology of the Skidi Pawnee Indians of North America,* Ballena Press Anthropological Papers, no. 26 (Los Angeles, CA: Ballena Press, 1982), 50-51.
8. Clark Wissler, *Some Protective Designs of the Dakota,* Anthropological Papers of the American Museum of Natural History, vol. 1, part 2 (New York: American Museum of Natural History, 1907), 26.
9. J. Owen Dorsey, *A Study of Siouan Cults,* 11th Annual Report of the Bureau of American Ethnology (Washington, 1894).
10. George Bird Grinnell, "Pawnee Mythology," *Journal of American Folklore* 6, no. 21 (1893): 113-130, and George A. Dorsey, *The Cheyenne: Ceremonial Organization,* Field Columbian Museum, Publication No. 99, Anthropological Series, vol. 9, no. 1 (Chicago: Field Columbian Museum, 1905).
11. Peter J. Powell, *Sweet Medicine: The Continuing Role of the Sacred Arrows, the Sun Dance, and the Sacred Buffalo Hat in Northern Cheyenne History,* 2 vols. (Norman: University of Oklahoma Press, 1969), 2: 435,644.
12. Fred W. Voget, *The Shoshoni-Crow Sun Dance* (Norman: University of Oklahoma Press, 1984).
13. George Bird Grinnell, *The Cheyenne Indians,* 2 vols. (New Haven, Yale University Press, 1923), and Voget, *The Shoshoni-Crow Sundance.*
14. Chamberlain, *When Stars Came Down to Earth,* 25, 57, 222.
15. Ibid., 55.
16. Grinnell, *The Cheyenne Indians,* 2: 108.
17. Dorsey, *A Study of Siouan Cults,* 446.
18. Grinnell, *The Cheyenne Indians,* 2:110.
19. Mooney, *The Ghost Dance Religion.*
20. Ibid.
21. Ibid.
22. Ibid.
23. Ibid.
24. Brigham D. Madsen, *The Northern Shoshoni* (Caldwell, Idaho: Caxton printers, 1980), 198.
25. Mooney, *The Ghost Dance Religion,* 51.
26. Ibid.
27. Madsen, *The Northern Shoshoni,* 198.
28. Ibid.
29. Mooney, *The Ghost Dance Religion,* 29.
30. Ibid., 35.
31. George A. Dorsey, *The Arapaho Sundance: The Ceremony of the Offerings Lodge,* Field Columbian Museum Publication, no. 75, Anthropological Series, vol. 4 (Chicago: Field Columbian Museum, 1903); Dorsey, *The Cheyenne: Ceremonial Organization;* Grinnell, *The Cheyenne Indians;* and Powell, *Sweet Medicine.*
32. Powell, *Sweet Medicine,* 1:5.
33. Ibid., 2:435.
34. David Wooley, "The Ghost Dance—A Pan-Indian Movement? Another View: Adaptation and Change" (Paper presented at the 14th Annual Plains Indian Seminar, Buffalo Bill Historical Center, Cody, Wyoming, September, 1990).
35. Dorsey, *The Arapaho Sun Dance.*
36. Ibid.
37. Howard L. Harrod, *Renewing the World: Plains Indian Religion and Morality* (Tucson: University of Arizona Press, 1987), 51, and Dorsey, *The Arapaho Sun Dance.*
38. Dorsey, *The Arapaho Sun Dance,* 12.
39. Ibid.
40. Ibid.
41. Mooney, *The Ghost Dance Religion.*
42. Powell, *Sweet Medicine,* 2:784.
43. David Wooley and William Waters, "Wa-No-She's Dance," *American Indian Art Magazine* 14, no. 1 (Winter 1988): 36-45.

44. Mooney, *The Ghost Dance Religion;* Elaine Goodale Eastman, "The Ghost Dance War and the Wounded Knee Massacre of 1890-91." *Nebraska History* 26 (1945): 26-42; Bob Lee, "Messiah Craze—Wounded Knee." *South Dakota Historical Society Bulletin* (May 1, 1955); David Humphreys Miller, *Ghost Dance.* (New York: Duel, Sloan and Pearce, 1959); Dee Brown, *Bury My Heart at Wounded Knee* (New York: Holt, Rinehart and Winston, 1971).

45. Mooney, *The Ghost Dance Religion,* 19.
46. Trudy Thomas, "Crisis and Creativity: Visual Symbolism of the Ghost Dance Tradition" (Ph.D. dissertation, Columbia University, 1988).
47. Harrod, *Renewing the World,* 171.

BIBLIOGRAPHY
(Thomas)

Brown, Dee. *Bury My Heart at Wounded Knee.* New York: Holt, Rinehart and Winston, 1971.

Chamberlain, Von Del. *When Stars Came Down to Earth: Cosmology of the Skidi Pawnee Indians of North America.* Ballena Press Anthropological Papers, No. 26. (Los Angeles, CA: Ballena Press), 1982.

Christiansen, Palle. *The Melanesian Cargo Cult: Millenarianism as a Factor in Cultural Change.* (Published for the Institute of Ethnology and Anthropology, University of Copenhagen). Copenhagen: Akademisk Forlag, 1969.

Dorsey, J. Owen. *A Study of Siouan Cults.* 11th Annual Report, Bureau of American Ethnology. Washington, 1894.

Dorsey, George A. *The Arapaho Sun Dance: The Ceremony of the Offerings Lodge.* Field Columbian Museum. Publication No. 75. Anthropological Series, vol. 4. Chicago: Field Columbian Museum, 1903.

Dorsey, George A. *The Cheyenne: Ceremonial Organization.* Field Columbian Museum. Publication No. 99. Anthropological Series, vol. 9, no. 1. Chicago: Field Columbian Museum, 1905.

Eastman, Elaine Goodale. "The Ghost Dance War and the Wounded Knee Massacre of 1890-91." *Nebraska History* 26 (1945): 26-42.

Ewers, John Canfield. *Plains Indian Painting.* Stanford, Ca.: Stanford University Press, 1939.

Ewers, John Canfield. "Plains Indian Painting: The History and Development of an American Art Form" *American West* 5, no. 2 (1968): 4-15, 74-75.

Fletcher, Alice C. and Francis La Fleche. *The Omaha Tribe.* 27th Annual Report of the Bureau of American Ethnology. Washington, D.C.: GPO, 1911.

Grinnell, George Bird. "Pawnee Mythology." *Journal of American Folklore* 6, no. 21 (1893): 113-130.

Grinnell, George Bird. *The Cheyenne Indians.* 2 vols. New Haven: Yale University Press, 1923.

Harrod, Howard L. *Renewing the World: Plains Indian Religion and Morality.* Tucson: University of Arizona Press, 1987.

Lee, Bob. "Messiah Craze—Wounded Knee." *South Dakota Historical Society Bulletin,* May 1, 1955.

Lesser, Alexander. "Cultural Significance of the Ghost Dance." *American Anthropologist* 35, no. 1 (1933): 108-115.

Lesser, Alexander. *The Pawnee Ghost Dance Hand Game: A Study in Cultural Change.* Columbia University Contributions in Anthropology, no. 16. New York: Columbia University Press, 1933.

Lowie, Robert H. *The Assiniboin.* Anthropological Papers of the American Museum of Natural History. Vol. 4, 1-169. New York: American Museum of Natural History, 1909.

Miller, David Humphreys. *Ghost Dance.* New York: Duel, Sloan and Pearce, 1959.

Madsen, Brigham D. *The Northern Shoshoni.* Caldwell, Idaho: Caxton Printers, 1980.

Minneapolis Institute of Arts. *I Wear the Morning Star: An Exhibition of American Indian Ghost Dance Objects.* Minneapolis, Minn: Minneapolis Institute of Arts, 1976.

Mooney, James. *The Ghost Dance Religion and the Sioux Outbreak of 1890.* Abridged, with an introduction by Anthony F.C. Wallace. Chicago: University of Chicago Press, 1965.

Pohrt, Richard A. "The Indian and the American Flag." *American Indian Art Magazine* 1, no. 2 (Spring 1976): 42-48.

Powell, Peter J. *Sweet Medicine: The Continuing Role of the Sacred Arrows, the Sun Dance, and the Sacred Buffalo Hat in Northern Cheyenne History.* 2 vols. Norman: University of Oklahoma Press, 1969.

Rodee, Howard D. "The Stylistic Development of Plains Indian Painting and Its Relationship to Ledger Drawings." *Plains Anthropologist* 10, no. 30 (November 1965).

Voget, Fred W. *The Shoshoni-Crow Sun Dance.* Norman: University of Oklahoma Press, 1984.

Wissler, Clark. *Some Protective Designs of the Dakota.* Anthropological Papers of the American Museum of Natural History. Vol. 1, part 2. New York: American Museum of Natural History, 1907.

Wissler, Clark. *Sun Dance of the Plains Indians.* Anthropological Papers of the American Museum of Natural History. Vol. 16. New York: American Museum of Natural History, 1921.

Wooley, David. "The Ghost Dance—A Pan-Indian Movement? Another View: Adaptation and Change." Paper presented at the 14th Annual Plains Indian Seminar, Buffalo Bill Historical Center, Cody, Wyoming, September, 1990.

Wooley, David and William Waters. "Wa-No-She's Dance." *American Indian Art Magazine* 14, no. 1 (Winter 1988): 36-45.

MASSACRE AT WOUNDED KNEE, 1890: DESCENDANTS OF INDIAN SURVIVORS SPEAK
Jeanne Eder

NOTES

1. Frederick E. Hoxie, *Indians in American History* (Arlington Heights, Illinois: Harlan Davidson, Inc., 1988), 15.
2. Abraham Chapman, ed., *Literature of the American Indians: Views and Interpretations* (New York: New American Library, 1975), 103.
3. John Tosh, *The Pursuit of History* (New York: Longman Group, 1984), 182.
4. Jessie Kills Close to the Lodge Crow, interview by Claudia Iron Hawk Sully, 1990, 1.
5. Calvin Jumping Bull, interview by Emma Iron Plume Clifford, 1990, 3.
6. Claudia Iron Hawk Sully, interview by Emma Iron Plume Clifford, 1990.

7. United States. Department of the Interior. *First, Second, and Third Annual Reports of the United States Geological Survey of the Territories for the Years 1867, 1868, and 1869,* by F.V. Hayden (Washington: Government Printing Office, 1873), 63.
8. Robert M. Utley, *The Last Days of the Sioux Nation* (New Haven: Yale University Press, 1963), 41.
9. James C. Olson, *Red Cloud and the Sioux Problem* (Lincoln: University of Nebraska Press, 1965), 105-106.
10. Leonard Little Finger, interview by Mike Her Many Horses, 1990, 3.
11. Chief Eagle, interview by Emma Iron Plume Clifford, 1990, 1.
12. Utley, *The Last Days of the Sioux Nation,* 31.
13. Ibid., 65.
14. Ibid., 66-70.
15. Francis He Crow, interview by Emma Iron Plume Clifford, 1990, 2-3.
16. Vine Deloria, Jr., *Behind the Trail of Broken Treaties* (Austin: University of Texas Press, 1985), 254.
17. Alex White Plume, interview by Emma Iron Plume Clifford, 1990, 2.
18. Deloria, *Behind the Trail of Broken Treaties,* 65.
19. Lawson Iron Hawk, interview by Emma Iron Plume Clifford, 1990, 1.
20. Ibid., 2.
21. Jumping Bull, interview, 1.
22. Chief Eagle, interview, 1.
23. Ralph K. Andrist, *The Long Death* (New York: Collier Books, 1964), 350.
24. Robert M. Utley, *The Indian Frontier of the American West 1846-1890* (Albuquerque: University of New Mexico Press, 1989), 256-257.
25. Rachel Hollow Horn, interview by Emma Iron Plume Clifford, 1990, 1.
26. Jumping Bull, interview, 1.
27. Lawson Iron Hawk, interview by Emma Iron Plume Clifford, 1990, 2.
28. Phoebe Iron Hawk-Red Elk, interview by Emma Iron Plume Clifford, 1990, 1.
29. Utley, *The Indian Frontier of the American West 1846-1890,* 256-257.
30. Ibid., 216.
31. Iron Hawk, interview, 2.
32. Steven Good Crow, interview by Claudia Iron Hawk Sully, 1990, 1.
33. Jumping Bull, interview, 2.
34. Iron Hawk-Red Elk, interview, 1.
35. Little Finger, interview, 1.
36. Ibid., 1-2.
37. Ibid., 2.
38. Ibid., 2.
39. Deloria, *Behind the Trail of Broken Treaties,* 67.
40. Utley, *The Last Days of the Sioux Nation,* 4.
41. Bernice Eagle Hawk White Hawk, interview by Emma Iron Plume Clifford, 1990, 1.
42. Utley, *The Last Days of the Sioux Nation,* 5.
43. Little Finger, interview, 1.
44. Clement C. High Hawk, interview by Emma Iron Plume Clifford, 1990, 1.
45. Elie Wiesel, "The Holocaust as Literary Inspiration," *Dimensions of the Holocaust, A Series of Lectures Presented at Northwestern University.* (Evanston, Illinois: Northwestern University, 1977) 33.
46. Raymond Pipe on Head, interview by Claudia Iron Hawk Sully, 1990, 1.
47. Claudia Iron Hawk Sully, interview by Emma Iron Plume Clifford, 1990, 1.
48. Utley, *The Last Days of the Sioux Nation,* 249-250.
49. Eugene White Hawk, interview by Emma Iron Plume Clifford, 1990, 1.
50. Ibid., 2.
51. Tex Broken Nose, interview by Emma Iron Plume Clifford, 1990, 1.
52. Daniel Afraid of Hawk, interview by Emma Iron Plume Clifford, 1990, 1.
53. Orval Looking Horse, interview by Emma Iron Plume Clifford, 1990, 1.
54. Robert McFee Brown, ed., *Elie Wiesel: Messenger to All Humanity* (London: University of Notre Dame Press, 1983), 20.

BIBLIOGRAPHY
(Eder)

Andrist, Ralph K. *The Long Death.* New York: Collier Books, 1964.

Brown, Robert McFee, ed. *Elie Wiesel: Messenger to All Humanity.* London: University of Notre Dame Press, 1983.

Chapman, Abraham, ed. *Literature of the American Indians: Views and Interpretations.* New York: New American Library, 1975.

Deloria, Vine, Jr. *Behind the Trail of Broken Treaties.* Austin: University of Texas Press, 1985.

United States. Department of the Interior. *First, Second, and Third Annual Reports of the United States Geological Survey of the Territories, For the Years 1867, 1868, and 1869,* by V.F. Hayden. Washington: Government Printing Office, 1873.

Hoxie, Frederick E. *Indians in American History.* Arlington Heights, Illinois: Harlan Davidson, Inc., 1988.

Olson, James C. *Red Cloud and the Sioux Problem.* Lincoln: University of Nebraska Press, 1965.

The Weekly Missoulian. September 2, 1874. No. 25.

Tosh, John. *The Pursuit of History.* New York: Longman Group, 1984.

Utley, Robert M. *The Last Days of the Sioux Nation.* New Haven: Yale University Press, 1963.

Utley, Robert M. *The Indian Frontier of the American West 1846-1890.* Albuquerque: University of New Mexico Press, 1984.

Wiesel, Elie. "The Holocaust As Literary Inspiration." *Dimensions of the Holocaust, A Series of Lectures Presented at Northwestern University.* Coordinated by the Department of History. Evanston, Illinois: Northwestern University, 1977.

Personal Interviews:

Afraid of Hawk, Daniel. Interview by Emma Iron Plum Clifford, 1990.

Bear Shield, Matthew Zack. Interview by Claudia Iron Hawk Sully, 1990.

Broken Nose, Tex. Interview by Emma Iron Plume Clifford, 1990.

Chief Eagle. Interview by Emma Iron Plume Clifford, 1990.

Eagle Hawk White Hawk, Bernice. Interview by Emma Iron Plume Clifford, 1990.

Good Crow, Steven. Interview by Claudia Iron Hawk Sully, 1990.

He Crow, Francis. Interview by Emma Iron Plume Clifford, 1990.

High Hawk, Clement C. Interview by Emma Iron Plume Clifford, 1990.

Hollow Horn, Adolph. Interview by Emma Iron Plume Clifford, 1990.

Hollow Horn, Rachel. Interview by Emma Iron Plume Clifford, 1990.

Horn Cloud, William. Interview by Emma Iron Plume Clifford, 1990.

Iron Hawk, Lawson. Interview by Emma Iron Plume Clifford, 1990.

Iron Hawk-Red Elk, Phoebe. Interview by Emma Iron Plume Clifford, 1990.
Jumping Bull, Calvin. Interview by Emma Iron Plume Clifford, 1990.
Kills Close to the Lodge Crow, Jessie. Interview by Claudia Iron Hawk Sully, 1990.
Little Finger, Leonard. Interview by Mike Her Many Horses, 1990.
Looking Horse, Orval. Interview by Emma Iron Plume Clifford, 1990.
Pipe on Head, Raymond. Interview by Claudia Iron Hawk, 1990.
Sully, Claudia Iron Hawk. Interview by Emma Iron Plume Clifford, 1990.
Weasel Bear Martin, Nancy. Interview by Claudia Iron Hawk Sully, 1990.
White Hawk, Eugene. Interview by Emma Iron Plume Clifford, 1990.
White Plume, Alex. Interview by Emma Iron Plume Clifford, 1990.

ABOUT THE AUTHORS

Alvin M. Josephy, Jr.

A well-known author, editor and historian, Alvin M. Josephy, Jr. has a longstanding interest in the history and condition of the American Indian. Mr. Josephy has pursued a varied career as a reporter, news director, combat correspondent, screen writer, and editor. He is the author of numerous award-winning magazine articles and books on Indian affairs, U.S. and Western history, and environmental subjects. *Now That the Buffalo's Gone: A Study of Today's American Indian*, is one of his most recent publications.

Trudy Thomas

Trudy Thomas is the Curator of Fine Art at the Museum of Northern Arizona, Flagstaff. She received a Ph.D. in Art History and Archaeology from Columbia University in 1988. In addition to curating many exhibits for the Museum of Northern Arizona she has served as consultant to the National Museum of Natural History, Smithsonian Institution, among others. Dr. Thomas brings a background in both anthropology and art history to her presentation of Ghost Dance material.

Jeanne Oyawin Eder

Jeanne Oyawin Eder is a doctoral candidate in history at Washington State University in Pullman. After receiving an M.A. in history at Montana State University, she taught Native American Studies at Eastern Montana College in Billings, Montana, for seven years. An enrolled member of the Assiniboine and Sioux tribes and born on the Ft. Peck reservation in Montana, Ms. Eder is interested in collecting Native American oral histories, working with museums and writing the histories of Northern Plains Indians. Her interests have resulted in the development and stage presentation of a portrayal of the historical Hidatsa character Waheenee, Buffalo Bird Woman.

ILLUSTRATION AND EXHIBITION CHECKLIST

1. *Quirt or Dance Wand, Cheyenne/Arapaho, c. 1891.* Loaned by the Cleveland Museum of Natural History, 8514. Photo: BBHC
Similar items with similar designs can also be observed in non-Ghost Dance ceremonies. Page 1.

2. *Shirt, deerskin, Arapaho, c. 1890.* Chandler/Pohrt Collection, Buffalo Bill Historical Center, Cody, Wyoming. Photo: BBHC
A classic garment featuring many key symbols of the Ghost Dance: the five-pointed stars, the turtle, the magpies, and the crows. Crows are birds that represent departed spirits. A red, human figure is on the tab of this shirt. Page 2.

3. *Ball, Arapaho, c. 1900.* Field Museum of Natural History, Chicago. Photo: BBHC.
A turtle ball decorated with a breathe feather of an eagle. There are many symbols incorporated into this turtle. Page 4.

4. *Shield, muslin, Sioux, c. 1890.* Private Collection. Photo: BBHC.
The circular frame of this shield is formed by willows. Page 4.

5. *Rattle, Apache, c. 1890.* Oklahoma Historical Society, State Museum of History, Oklahoma City. Photo: BBHC.
A crescent representing the celestial body as well as what might be a rainbow are pressed into this rawhide rattle. Page 5.

6. *Dress, deerskin, Arapaho, c. 1885.* Albert Green Heath Collection. Logan Museum of Anthropology, Beloit College, Wisconsin. Photo: BBHC.
Feathered birds are a vital element of the Ghost Dance. Here we see a feathered dress about to take flight. Page 5.

7. *Dress, muslin, Arapaho, c. 1890 (?).* Montana Private Collection. Photo: Courtesy of Collector.
It has been theorized that the more basic and simple patterns emerged from the 1890 Ghost Dance, whereas more intricate patterns, as shown here, may have come from a later time, perhaps drawn for the reenactment. But this is only theory. Page 6.

8. *Horned Bonnet, Northern Plains, c. 1840.* Irving H. "Larry" Larom Collection, Buffalo Bill Historical Center, Cody, Wyoming. Photo: BBHC. Page 6.

9. *Karl Bodmer, 1809-1893. Noapeh an Assiniboin Indian, Psihdja-Sahpa a Yankton Indian, 1840-43,* (detail depicting Noapeh). Engraving and aquatint, hand colored, 18-1/8x24-7/8". From *Travels in the Interior of North America* by Prince Maximilian of Wied-Neuwied. Buffalo Bill Historical Center, Cody, Wyoming. Gift of Clara S. Peck. (*Catalogue illustration only.*) Photo: BBHC. Page 6.

10. *Saddle Blanket, Northern Plains, c. 1840.* Chandler/Pohrt Collection. Photo: BBHC.
A partially reconstructed pre-1850 Northern Plains saddle blanket. Close scrutiny will reveal the new materials. Repairs are reversible. From the three remaining tin cones it was determined that the tufts held woven cloth instead of horsehair or yarn. Page 7.

11. *Dress, muslin, Sioux, c. 1890.* Museum of the Great Plains, Lawton, Oklahoma. Photo: BBHC.
A bald eagle in the heavens is shown on this muslin dress. Page 8.

12. *Entrance to Mass Burial Grave, Wounded Knee Cemetery.* Photo: BBHC
The grave is the open area in the center. Page 9.

13. *Pennant, company guidon.* From the Hayes Otoupalik Collection. Photo: BBHC. Page 10.

14. *U.S. Army Soldier dressed for winter on the Plains, c. 1890.*
Muskrat Cap, U.S. Army, model 1876, From the Hayes Outapalik Collection; *Buffalo Hide Coat,* military style, c. 1880. Buffalo Bill Museum, Buffalo Historical Center, Original Collection; *Cavalry Boots,* U.S. Army, model 1884. From the Hayes Outapalik Collection; *U.S. Springfield Infantry Rifle,* .45-70 caliber, model 1873. Cody Firearms Museum, Buffalo Bill Historical Center. Photo: BBHC. Page 11.

15. *Shirt, deerskin, Pawnee, c. 1890.* Grand Teton National Park. Photo: BBHC.
These symbols are truly a mixture of Christian, Ghost Dance and perhaps other philosophies, but all spiritual in nature. Page 15.

16. *Bustle, Arapaho, c. 1885.* Crane Collection, Department of Anthropology, Denver Museum of Natural History. Photo: BBHC.
A rare and special item that establishes the connection with older items being incorporated into the Ghost Dance. Page 15.

17. *Dress, deerskin, Southern Plains, c. 1890 (?).* Collection of Richard and Nedra Matteucci. Photo: Courtesy of Richard and Nedra Matteucci. Page 16.

18. *Seventh Cavalry, Wounded Knee, c. 1890.* Photographer — Clarence Grant Morledge. Courtesy of the Denver Public Library, Western History Department, Denver, Colorado. Page 18.

19. *Sitting Bull, c. 1883.* Photographer — David F. Barry. Courtesy Paul and Teresa Harbaugh. Page 19.

20. *Indian Policemen. c. 1890 (?).* Photographer — David F. Barry. Courtesy of the Denver Public Library, Western History Department, Denver, Colorado. (*Catalogue illustration only.*) The man in the center is Red Tomahawk. Page 19.

21. *Sitting Bull's Cane, Sioux, c. 1885.* Robinson State Museum, South Dakota State Historical Society, Pierre. Photo: BBHC.
The personal cane of a great man, made from diamond willow. Page 19.

22. *Jacket, man's, Sioux, c. 1890.* America Hurrah, New York City. Photo: BBHC.
This jacket was purchased for the colorful quillwork that was on the outside. Noting that the lining was torn, painted areas could be seen inside. After removing the lining, the painted Ghost Dance motif was readily apparent. Perhaps to conceal the Ghost Dance motif after the movement became unpopular, the owner turned the jacket inside out and applied quillwork on the new exterior. Page 20.

23. *General Brooke's Camp, Pine Ridge Agency, c. 1891.* Photographer — Clarence Grant Morledge. Courtesy Paul and Teresa Harbaugh. Page 22.

24. *Hotchkiss Cannon, American Ordnance #104.* From the Hayes Otoupalik Collection. Photo: BBHC.
Guns of this type were extensively used by the U.S. Army in the West. Page 24.

25. *Winchester Model 1866 carbine .44 caliber.* Cody Firearms Museum, Buffalo Bill Historical Center, Cody, Wyoming. Photo: BBHC.
The Model 1866 was extremely popular not only with western emigrants, but also Native Americans. Page 24.

26. *Hotchkiss Shell,* caliber 1.65", high explosive impact fragmentation round. From the Hayes Otoupalik Collection. Page 25.

27. *Intrenching/Hunting Knife, U.S. Army, c. 1880.* From the Hayes Otoupalik Collection. Page 25.

28. *Gathering Up the Dead at the Battlefield at Wounded Knee, S.D., 1891.* Photographer — Clarence Grant Morledge. Courtesy of the Smithsonian Institution. Page 26.

29. *Chief Big Foot's Knife, c. 1880.* Robinson State Museum, South Dakota State Historical Society, Pierre. Photo: BBHC. Page 26.

30. *Sioux Indian War Medal, Nebraska State National Guard, 1890-1891 (left), Congressional Medal of Honor, undesignated, c. 1890 (middle), Indian War Medal with matching chest ribbon (right).* From the Hayes Otoupalik Collection.
The existence of such medals clearly demonstrates that the Indians at the time were considered great enemies of the republic and men were rewarded by the state and nation for fighting and killing them. Page 27.

31. *Kicking Bear, Young Man Afraid, Standing Bear, Pine Ridge Agency, January 1891.* Photographer — Clarence Grant Morledge. Courtesy of the Denver Public Library, Western History Department, Denver, Colorado. Page 27.

32. *Sioux Family, c. 1890*
Sioux Man: *Warbonnet*, Irving H. "Larry" Larom Collection; *Shirt*, C.C. Moseley Collection; *Leggings*, Dr. Robert L. Anderson Collection; *Moccasins*, Richard A. Pohrt Collection.
Sioux Woman: *Dress*, Mrs. Henry H.R. Coe Collection; *Belt*, Mrs. Henry H.R. Coe Collection; *Moccasins*, Richard A. Pohrt Collection; *Leggings*, Robert F. Garland Collection.
Sioux Boy: *Vest*, Henriette S. Horton Collection; *Trousers*, Henriette S. Horton Collection; *Moccasins*, Harriet D. Reed and Betty N. Landercasper Collection.
Photo: BBHC, Shrikhande.
Developing from pre-1850 styles, prior to depreciating after the turn-of-the-century, the 1890 period is viewed as the zenith of traditional Plains Indian Art in quality and number. Here we see the styles of this period represented by the three-member family wearing their finest. Page 28.

33. *Dress, muslin, Sioux, c. 1885.* Courtesy of the National Museum of the American Indian, Smithsonian Institution. Photo: BBHC.
Here we see power coming from the bird's wing as that is one source of the bird's strength. Page 28.

34. *Dress, deerskin, Arapaho/Southern Plains, c. 1890.* Nichols Collection, Buffalo Bill Historical Center, Cody, Wyoming. Photo: BBHC.
It is said that the little lines with the balls on the ends may be a way to note time. Page 29.

35. *Dress, deerskin, Arapaho, c. 1890.* Eiteljorg Museum of American Indian and Western Art, Indianapolis, Indiana. Photo: BBHC.
One of the most beautiful Ghost Dance dresses in the world. The bottom part of a dress is usually made with the flesh side out, whereas the top part has the hair side out. One can only speculate on the meaning of the symbols, but a jagged line is often the route of power and the large circle may be the sun. Page 30.

36. *Shirt, muslin, Sioux, c. 1890.* Courtesy of the National Museum of the American Indian, Smithsonian Institution. Photo: BBHC.
This shirt is decorated with drawings identical to those used by Catlin many years earlier. The reasons for the drawing are unknown. Page 31.

37. *Shirt, muslin, Gros Ventre, 50/4320, c. 1890.* American Museum of Natural History, New York, New York. Photo: BBHC.
This shirt is the most colorful and all-encompassing painted muslin shirt of its kind. It was created by a tribe little known for their activities in the Ghost Dance. Page 31.

38. *Leggings, men's, Arapaho, c. 1890.* Eiteljorg Museum of American Indian and Western Art, Indianapolis, Indiana. Photo: BBHC. Page 31.

39. *Star Hair Ornament, Arapaho, c. 1890 (?).* Montana, Private Collection. Photo: BBHC.
Cut and dyed feathers augment the silver star in this hair ornament. Page 32.

40. *Dress, deerskin, Arapaho, pre-1903.* Field Museum of Natural History, Chicago. Photo: BBHC. Page 32.

41. *Shirt, deerskin, Kiowa, c. 1890.* Lowie Museum of Anthropology, University of California Berkeley. Photo: BBHC.
The Indian artist often determines a fundamental truth of an object, symbolizes it and then utilizes that symbol in various manners and shapes. Here we see the rainbow used in many different forms and shapes that attest to a new day and the end of a storm. Page 33.

42. *Wovoka, Ghost Dance Prophet, c. 1921.* Courtesy Nevada State Historical Society, Reno, Nevada.
(*Catalogue illustration only.*) Page 33.

43. *Feathers, golden eagle, painted, Kiowa, c. 1890.*
The Fort Sill Museum, Fort Sill, Oklahoma. Photo: BBHC.
These feathers are symbolic because they have experienced some hard times since their initial conception, but they still represent great beauty in material and belief. Page 34.

44. *Dress, muslin, Sioux, 50/3054, c. 1890.* American Museum of Natural History. Photo: BBHC.
The element over the bird is said to represent a four-pointed abstract star and below we see butterflies and buffalo hoof prints as well as other stars. Page 34.

45. *Dress, deerskin, Arapaho, c. 1885.* Courtesy of the National Museum of the American Indian, Smithsonian Institution. Photo: BBHC.
One of the most highly decorated and beautiful Ghost Dance dresses in the world. The eagles, rainbows, cedar trees, and other symbols can be seen on many Ghost Dance items, but the rabbit is special. The Arapaho people admire the rabbit not only for its quickness and agility, but also for its peaceful nature. Page 35.

46. *Tobacco bag, Arapaho, c. 1890 (?).* Montana, Private Collection. Photo: BBHC.
Indian people utilized symbols of animals they respected in the hope of obtaining some of the animals' powers. Here we can see turtles renowned for their tenacity to cling to life and their ability to attain great age. Page 36.

47. *Dress, canvas flag, Southern Plains, c. 1890 (?).* Mr. and Mrs. Forrest Fenn, Santa Fe, New Mexico. Photo: Courtesy Mr. and Mrs. Forrest Fenn. An extraordinary dress cut in the Southern Plains style made from a flag and canvas materials. Page 36.

48. *Claudia Iron Hawk Sully, president, Wounded Knee Survivors Association. Wounded Knee, South Dakota, 1990.* Photo: BBHC (*Catalogue illustration only.*) Page 38.

49. *Villa of Brule, 1891.* Photographer — John C.H. Grabill. Courtesy Paul and Teresa Harbaugh (*Catalogue illustration only.*) Page 39.

50. *Shield, Arapaho, c. 1890.* Collection of the Portland Art Museum of the Oregon Art Institute. Gift of Elizabeth Cole Butler. Photo: BBHC.
Seven was a favorite number among many tribes and animals, such as this antelope which was their food supply, also decorated select items. Page 41.

51. *Tobacco bag, Arapaho, c. 1880.* Chandler/Pohrt Collection, Buffalo Bill Historical Center, Cody, Wyoming. Photo: BBHC.
This man holding a cedar tree branch is another common motif in the Ghost Dance religion. The magpie was a favorite among the Paiute people where the religion originated. Page 42.

52. *Famous Battery E, Wounded Knee.* Photographer — Clarence Grant Morledge. Courtesy of the Denver Public Library, Western History Department, Denver, Colorado. Page 43.

53. *Colt Model 1873, Single Action Revolver, .45 caliber.* Cody Firearms Museum, Buffalo Bill Historical Center, Cody, Wyoming. Photo: BBHC.
The Model 1873 Colt Single Action Army Revolver was the standard U.S. Army sidearm from 1873 to 1900. Page 44.

54. *Sword and Scabbard, c. 1864.* Buffalo Bill Museum, Original Collection, Buffalo Bill Historical Center, Cody, Wyoming. Photo: BBHC. Page 44.

55. *Bird's-eye view of the Canyon at Wounded Knee, 1891.* Photographer — George E. Trager. Courtesy Paul and Teresa Harbaugh. Page 45.

56. *Doll, Sioux, c. 1890.* Museum of the Great Plains, Lawton, Oklahoma. Photo: BBHC.
This doll holds a number of common motifs of the Plains people, some of which may be related to the Ghost Dance such as the stars on the legs, the bird and perhaps the cedar tree. Page 46.

57. *Burial of the (Indian) dead at Wounded Knee, January 1, 1891.* Photographer — George E. Trager. Courtesy of the Smithsonian Institution. Page 47.

58. *Leaders of the Hostiles, Pine Ridge Agency, January 1891.* Photographer — Clarence Grant Morledge. Courtesy of the Denver Public Library, Western History Department, Denver, Colorado. Page 48.

59. *Monument at the Mass Grave, Wounded Knee Cemetery.* Photo: BBHC. Page 48.

60. *The Mass Grave, Wounded Knee Cemetery.* Photo: BBHC. Page 49.

61. *Proud Young Rider Holding Photograph of Rider. Pine Ridge Reservation.* Photo: BBHC. Page 50.

62. *Wounded Knee Site Today.* Photo: BBHC. Page 51.

63. *Ghost Dance, c. 1893.* Photographer — James Mooney. Courtesy of the National Anthropological Archives, Smithsonian Institution (*Catalogue illustration only.*) Page 60.

64. *Indians Forming Circle for Ghost Dance,* Native American Painting Reference Library, Private Collection. (*Not illustrated.*) This ledger drawing of related activities on the Southern Plains clearly shows feathers favored by some tribes for this ceremony.

65. *Lying Prostrate from Excitement in Ghost Dance.* Ledger drawing. Native American Painting Reference Library. Private Collection. (*Not illustrated.*)

66. *Untitled* (Dancers in a circle), Ledger drawing. Native American Painting Reference Library. Private Collection. (*Not illustrated.*)

67. *Circle in Ghost Dance.* Ledger Drawing. Native American Painting Reference Library. Private Collection. (*Not illustrated.*)

68. *Chief Big Foot's Hat, c. 1885.* Robinson State Museum, South Dakota State Historical Society, Pierre. (*Not illustrated.*) Chief Big Foot at one time was known as Spotted Elk.

69. *Short Bull's moccasins, Sioux, c. 1885.* Richard A. Pohrt Collection, Buffalo Bill Historical Center. (*Not illustrated.*) Short Bull was one of the primary leaders of the Sioux Ghost Dance. Before the days of cattle, the term 'Bull' referred to the male buffalo. So, when this name is utilized in Indian terms, it means buffalo bull.

70. *Shirt, muslin, Sioux, c. 1885.* Collection of the Denver Art Museum, Museum Purchase. (*Not illustrated.*) Power is coming out of the bird's mouth.

71. *Dress, muslin, Sioux, c. 1890.* Crane Collection, Department of Anthropology, Denver Museum of Natural History. (*Not illustrated.*)
Muslin is an inexpensive cotton cloth and usually the base material for the Ghost Dance clothing on the Northern Plains. However, all muslin clothing is not related to the Ghost Dance.

72. *Shirt, deerskin, Arapaho, c. 1885.* Eiteljorg Museum of American Indian and Western Art, Indianapolis, Indiana. (*Not illustrated.*)

73. *Shirt, deerskin, Arapaho, c. 1890.* Lent by the Kendall Young Library, Webster City, Iowa. (*Not illustrated.*) The fringe on Plains Indian shirts always falls on the back of the arm.

74. *Officers of 1st Infantry, c. 1891.* Photographer—Clarence Grant Morledge. Courtesy of the Denver Public Library, Western History Department, Denver, Colorado. (*Not illustrated.*)

75. *Ghost Dance before 1890.* Photographer Unknown. Courtesy of the National Anthropological Archives, Smithsonian Institution. (*Not illustrated.*)

76. *Street Scene, Pine Ridge Agency, c. 1890-1891.* Photographer—Clarence Grant Morledge. Courtesy of the Denver Public Library, Western History Department, Denver, Colorado. (*Not illustrated.*)

77. Karl Bodmer, 1809-1893. *Horse Racing of Sioux Indians Near Fort Pierre, 1840-43.* Engraving. 18-1/8x24-7/8". From *Travels in the Interior of North America* by Prince Maximilian of Wied-Neuwied. Buffalo Bill Historical Center, Cody, Wyoming. Gift of Clara S. Peck. (*Not illustrated.*)

Lenders to the Exhibition

Albert Green Heath Collection, Logan Museum of Anthropology, Beloit College
America Hurrah
American Museum of Natural History
The Cleveland Museum of Natural History
Crane Collection, Department of Anthropology, Denver Museum of Natural History
Denver Art Museum
Denver Public Library, Western History Department
Eiteljorg Museum of American Indian and Western Art
Mr. and Mrs. Forrest Fenn
Field Museum of Natural History
The Fort Sill Museum, Fort Sill
Grand Teton National Park
Hampton University Museum
Paul and Teresa Harbaugh
Hayes Otoupalik Collection
Kendall Young Library
Lowie Museum of Anthropology, University of California at Berkeley
Collection of Richard and Nedra Matteucci
Museum of the Great Plains
National Museum of the American Indian, Smithsonian Institution
Native American Painting Reference Library. Private Collection
Oklahoma Historical Society, State Museum of History
Richard A. Pohrt Collection
Collection of the Portland Art Museum of the Oregon Art Institute, Gift of Elizabeth Cole Butler
Private Collectors
Robinson State Museum, South Dakota State Historical Society

63. *Ghost Dance, c. 1893.*